Live

The Last Book You'll Ever Write

NATHAN KESSLER

Copyright © 2016 Nathan Kessler

All rights reserved.

ISBN-10: 1522791590
ISBN-13: 978-1522791591

DEDICATION

To my parents, Steve and Robin, who give me unconditional love and support.

Also to my brothers, Barry and Danny, who inspire me daily to be my best and set a great example.

CONTENTS

ACKNOWLEDGMENTS i

INTRODUCTION: PICK UP THE PEN(S) 3

YOU DON'T HAVE TO BE IN CHARGE TO BE A LEADER 8

START WITH GOOD ENOUGH 31

THE STYROFOAM ELEPHANT IN THE ROOM 38

FACING THE BITE 46

LOST, YET KNOWING EXACTLY WHERE YOU ARE 55

GET OFF THE SIDELINES 66

KARMA'S ADVANTAGE 74

IMPROVISE! 82

FORTY THOUSAND DOLLARS? OR FORTY BUCKS? 88

DO HARD THINGS 99

ACT WITH TACT 105

INVESTING IN DREAMS 114

MAKE THE MOST 121

IF YOU TRUST	128
UNPLUGGED YET CONNECTED	135
THE GRIND	141
NATURE > CONSEQUENCES	147
AM I HEADED IN *MY* DIRECTION?	152
OPEN MIND, OPEN WORLD	158
ONLY SO MUCH	166
KEEP THE PLANT RUNNING	173
"CHECK IN" TO REAL LIFE	178
DON'T BE A STRANGER	183
ENDLESS LEARNING	189
STORIES WORTH WRITING, STORIES WORTH READING	198
CONCLUSION: YOUR INTRODUCTION	205

ACKNOWLEDGMENTS

Glen Mescher, my old project manager, that crazy old man who taught me *real* work ethic. All the stories you've shared with me on the road—and always remind me to, *"Write that s*** down!"*

Loral Langemier, who nearly forced me to come to her "3 Days to Cash" seminar, where I pre-sold several copies of my book—which inspired me to finish it. Who taught me to say YES to my idea, and then figure it out.

And my good friend and publisher, Joshua Lisec, who has helped tremendously every step of the process. Who operates his life with a similar mindset to mine. Who allowed my stories to be brought to their full potential.

INTRODUCTION: PICK UP THE PEN(S)

What kind of life do you want to live?

When you're 80 years old, do you want to look back at your life and tell the stories of how you inspired hundreds of people to live more positive, productive lives and lift themselves out of poverty, went on months-long missions trips to uncontacted jungle tribes, and played a major role in ending the pollution of our country's waterways and drinking water?

Or do you want to tell the stories of how you spent your twenties and thirties binge-watching Netflix and reminiscing all the likes your Facebook statuses have gotten?

I ask you again; what kind of life do you want to live?

More importantly, what stories do you want to write through your life? What memories do you want to make?

Everyone loves a good story. But how many of us are actually living a good story—one that's more than just wake up/go to work/eat/watch TV/sleep/repeat?

I figure you've picked this book up because you're tired of volume after volume of self-help drivel, *"Here's a quote from Buddha and a picture of the ocean…"*

Here's what you're not going to get here. There aren't any 7 steps to happiness, 21 principles of inner peace, or 12 how-to's to manifest your desires.

This is all about you and your journey. Fulfillment is different for each individual, so I'll steer clear of the one-size-fits-all approach.

Back to stories. Your stories. The ones you're going to create, cherish, and tell the world. Stories that inspire people to take life-transforming action. Stories that bridge the gap between dreaming and doing.

Through this book, you will be guided to go the extra mile, take the leap, and do something crazy. You will be questioned, to question yourself.

You're going to be "writing your own chapters" by taking on daily challenges and journaling about your experiences, tracking your progress, and living an epic life worth writing your own book about—starting here, starting now.

As you progress through the chapters, you'll find the challenges getting tougher and tougher. Nobody said "the good life" was an easy one. Stories worth sharing aren't ones where the main character avoids the struggle.

Each story of mine that you read is intended to be a jumping-off point for you, or a spark of motivation. But do you really need my stories? Nope. But to live an epic life, we've all got to start somewhere.

Every lesson I've learned—no matter how silly or how eye-opening—is one I'm committed to passing on to you to spark some imagination to make your own stories more exciting, engaging, rich, and full of life and wonder.

Nobody wants to read the novel in which nothing ever happens. So why should you be content to live a life like that? Since we believe—no, we know—life is about more than just holding down a job and paying bills to maintain a middle class existence, you're going to be challenged in this book. At each chapter's end, you'll be expected to get up and write your own story—by living it.

You and I both need you to act on these lessons if you expect any change. I'd like to think of this as more of a life-shifting book, slamming you out of a neutral existence and accelerating your transformation into a top gear prodigy.

Because nothing is stopping us from doing what we've always wanted to do. Nothing is holding us back from our destiny. And no one is powerful enough to keep us from unlocking a life so exciting.

Except us—except you. Only your fearful hand can keep your life from shifting into the next gear.

We humans have a way of getting in our own way. The only way to knock down every obstacle and push through every barrier is to get yourself out of your own way.

Unconventional? Yep.

Effective? Turn the page, start reading, and find out for yourself.

You've got nothing to lose but boredom—forever.

YOU DON'T HAVE TO BE IN CHARGE TO BE A LEADER

You don't have to be in charge to be a leader. But you do have to make decisions like one.

"I quit. I just. I quit," moaned one of my co-workers. "If the boss ain't gonna pay us, I ain't gonna work." He whipped out a smoke and had a few puffs, while on the clock.

The project manager rushed past me while staring at some blueprints. "Look, I feel bad for you. And I don't blame you either. A hard day's work deserves a wage."

"A hard day?" spat a technician under his

breath. "More like a hard five weeks. My old lady is giving me hell 'cause I can't buy all the drugs and prescriptions we need. Afford all that out of pocket, no way. Do you even know what five weeks without health insurance does to your budget?"

"Make that back-pay with interest." The first employee whined. He ripped off his gloves and sat down with a magazine. "It's not like we're getting paid."

The project manager adjusted his faded baseball cap and shrugged. "He's definitely not gonna shoot it to us straight. I've been up to his office I can't tell you how many times. Always get the runaround. He's hopeless."

I slipped in my earbuds. Better to listen to a random podcast than the useless, unproductive, miniscule workroom b****ing for the umpteenth time this week. This two million dollar construction project for a museum was one of the biggest I'd tackled in my five years here, so I wasn't about to follow in their unproductivity.

This particular project was to be paid upon completion, meaning that the company didn't have enough money prior to taking on the project to pay employees until the project was complete. Thus, we the employees had gone over a month without getting paychecks.

Paid upon completion.

I knew it was paid upon completion, so it made sense to me to hurry up and finish it.

Don't even remember what I was doing.

But I do remember what I heard.

"Break time's almost here," I heard a muffled voice. Not even an episode of London Real could inoculate my ears from complaining that's gone viral. My locked car would be the break room of my choosing today, everyday really.

"I should just quit. Maybe complain to the state about it." The technician threw a drill onto the workbench beside me.

"You're not gonna quit," I jumped into the conversation, "because you want that paycheck. If it's really so bad here, then go get another job."

"We're all way too old to get a job somewhere else," replied the technician.

"You're full of great ideas, aren't you?"

said another co-worker. "I say we just walk right out the door and carpool our way down to job services. At least we'll get unemployment checks."

"Can't do that." The project manager snapped. "We're staying. Try to get some work done. Maybe he'll come around and decide to tell us what's up."

On my way to fetch screws from the shelves on the opposite side of the shop, I made sure to keep my eyes down. Bobbed my head, too. I figured that would be a clear enough sign that my ears were occupied with top forty hits. By the time I'd gotten what I needed and made the ten second walk back to my station, every employee and manager had camped out on the makeshift benches right next to where I needed to work. "Pre-break break," they called it.

"Hey, Nathan," the technician called to me, "turn that s*** off and join the club." This forced a chuckle from my co-workers.

"Yeah, it's not like you're on the clock," another added.

I hit pause.

I slammed my hammer on my bench to let my frustration be known—and to hopefully silence their useless whining. "How can you all sit here, day in and day out, crying about the circumstances, but never do anything about it?"

Silence. Everyone's gazes hit the floor.

"Here we sit on our a**es for what? Nothin', just nothin'. You all talk about quitting or going to job services, but none of you are going to do anything about it except complain to each other everyday come break time."

There had been talks of an early withdrawal on our payment, but the owner of the company couldn't give any details. And all the guys wanted was an answer.

"We're like mushrooms kept in the dark and fed s***." The painter shrugged. "You know, I've been here for nineteen years. I was the fifth employee here. Can't just walk out of here with that kind of record, but I don't see no point in sticking around."

"I'm going to go talk to the boss," I said confidently.

"Wouldn't do any good." The project manager kept his gaze to the grimy sawdust-covered floor.

"We want an answer. Why can't I ask for it?"

There must have been something special about that dusty, metal-shaving covered, oil slick-spotted floor because every guy's eyes were stuck on it. Just, stuck. I probably could've set a hundred dollar bill on fire and they wouldn't have noticed.

"You can't, Nate." The shop supervisor sighed. "We're just peons. We can't change this."

I felt my grip on my hammer loosen.

"Here it is, kid." The project manager finally looked up at me. "Your future. Just a bunch of old geezers crying about the circumstances but doing nothing about it. We can't control a damn thing."

Your future.

Those two words. Those two circumstantially s****y words.

Your future.

In fifteen years, I'd be thirty-eight. That's

a long-a** time. And I'd be spending every minute of it huddled between my project manager and supervisor, grumbling about whatever trouble the man in charge is stirring up. That sucks.

"Hey Nate, you might as well get back to work. Nothing's gonna change." The technician snickered. As if it were normal to live like this, and everything was okay.

I felt the strangest pulse rush through my hands. The hammer dropped.

He was right, and for a slight second I felt like I was one of them now. The longer any one of us waited to do something, the easier it was to do, well, nothing. You know what? That feeling is surprisingly comfortable—for a time.

I stared down the technician. "Okay. You're right. But not anymore." I slipped off my gloves, wiped my hands on my work shirt.

"Huh. What's gotten into you?" The technician rolled his eyes.

"Look at us. Seriously. I can't live with myself, knowing that the highest calling I've lived up to becoming one of you guys."

"Do you even know who you're talking to, punk?" The technician's crooked spine straightened up.

"Do you even know what you want?" I shrugged. "That goes for everyone. Do we even know what we want from the boss? Seriously, guys, what do we want? You complain about circumstances daily, but you never discuss the circumstances you really want?"

The project manager shook his head. "That's a good question. But I don't see how anything will change—"

"Nothing will change," I cut him off, "if you don't believe something will change."

"That's good, that's good." The shop supervisor sat up. "Well, who wants a Marlboro? Anybody got a light?"

Really? I was not about to let a hankering for a hit derail my future. Funny how you can tolerate indecisiveness for what seems like forever. Until you snap. Most people probably never do though. I guess I'm just not one of those people.

The project manager raised an eyebrow at

me, as if it to say, "Got a light?"

Now that my adrenaline-laced thoughts were out there for everybody, I'd look like a complete idiot if I didn't follow through. So I did.

I threw my safety glasses and tape measure onto the workbench and made a confident bolt for that accursed corner office.

The door was opened, so I walked right in and marched up to his cluttered, half-assembled desk.

"Hey Nathan." His head laid low. "Listen. I know the situation. We've talked about it before in the shop."

"They want answers. Now."

"I know, I know." The boss shook his head.

"The guys are pissed off, frustrated, and unproductive, and this is YOUR company image and income on the line."

He cleared his throat and tapped his keyboard a couple times. "Are they really that angry?"

"*5 weeks unpaid...DO YOU HAVE TO ASK!? Of course they are!*" I screamed in my head.

"Yep." I nodded. "A word from you might do us all some good."

"A word about what?" He finally looked me in the eye. "We get paid upon completion, including me. If that's what this is all about…"

"Yes," I said. "And no."

"What do you mean?" I could tell pride hid within his fearful tone.

It had to be broken. I knew what I wanted—and what my guys back in the shop needed.

"They just want you to be honest with them. They want an answer. From you. Personally."

"Nope, can't do that." He sunk back in his chair. "We're weeks behind schedule. I don't know how that happened, but here we are. What do they want me to do? Pay them out of my own pocket?"

That'd be nice.

Didn't say that. Instead I repeated my concern, "All they want is to hear it from you straight. What's the status of the job? They're all good workers. You know you don't hire slobs. We know we're going to get paid what we've earned. You're good for the money. The money is not the issue, they just want the truth. They don't mind working for free for now, so long as they know what's happening."

Moved by this bit of ego-stroking, he uncrossed his arms. "Sounds fair and square to me. But tell me. What makes you think they'd even want me to come down there?"

I guess I have to spell it out for this guy. "You know I listen to a lot of audiobooks and podcasts about high performance on the job, right?"

The boss shrugged. "Yeah, never got a complaint about it. Seems like they keep you focused."

"A couple weeks ago, I heard this story about the Nash Clothing Company down in Cincinnati. Several decades ago, they went from a profitable company to just plain broke. All of a sudden, they couldn't meet payroll. There was only one thing that could save the business."

I paused. "The employees. The plan the

owner created would inspire everyone to go all-in with their heart, soul, and wallet. And if it worked, everyone was going to get a serious payday."

I took another breath, letting my boss feel the pressure of silence. "The owner went straight to his employees and said, 'Look, I need to be honest with you. We've been sliding downhill, and I can't meet payroll this coming week. I don't know how long it will be until I can. There's been a lack of excitement and enthusiasm around here, I can tell. On Monday, if you're able to come in here with a positive attitude like you had when we first started, I think we can make it. I'll pay you your wages, plus everything I owe you in back pay. Together, I believe we can save the company. It's time to take a new lease on life.'"

I broke away from the story for a moment. "You know what effect that had on his employees?"

My boss just shrugged.

"When the owner got back from lunch," I continued, "he found $16,000 in cash laying on his desk. His employees felt so inspired by his honesty, that they pooled together their savings, their spending money, and rainy day cash to keep the business afloat. Because it was their business, too. The owner believed in them, so they believed in him. It wasn't long before the Nash Clothing Company was the most profitable mail order clothes retailer in the entire United States."

I finished my thoughts. "You see, all those people needed was for the leader to be a leader. And that meant being honest."

My boss stared at his computer monitor for a few seconds, his forehead wrinkled. "Guess I have something to say then. Go back out there. I need to prepare first."

I returned to my work station and tried to act semi-productive compared to "the crying circle."

About ten minutes later, the project manager did a double-take and sprang from his seat. "What brings you down here?"

"Hey," the boss said in a tender voice. "I know you guys want an update on the payment. Well, I'm waiting for that update, too. But that doesn't make it right for you to not have any answer at all about whether you're getting a paycheck on Friday. At the end of the day, you have all earned your paychecks, and it doesn't make it right." His head dropped. So did the tears. "I love you guys. We've got to make it past this point. And I believe in every one of you."

The man cried, pouring his heart and soul into his speech. The crew was touched, it hit home. Their faces said it all while they remained speechless.

At the end of his speech, the most irate employee was the first to offer a handshake and a compliment. "We'll get through this, don't worry about it. Thank you for being honest."

After a bunch of hugs and handshakes, productivity and b****ing had an inverse relationship. This time, it was in the company's best interest.

After shaking everyone else's hands, the boss shook mine—he really, really shook it. Like a real man. With tears in his eyes, he nodded his head and wagged a finger of recognition right at me. With a firm pat on my shoulder, he walked humbly back to his office. The burden, gone.

"Nathan!" the project manager shook his head, hiding back a chuckle, "what the hell did you do?"

I slipped my gloves back on, giving myself a couple seconds to think. *I made a decision. I said what needed to be heard.*

Most people are comfortable in their own misery. Do they have potential? Absolutely. Is there more out there than the daily grind, followed by happy hour? Probably. Have they become numb to their dreams? Definitely.

I don't think any kid wakes up and says, "When I grow up, I want to go to the same place every day. I want a paycheck that barely pays my bills. I want a sucky boss who has me b****ing all day long." But one day that kid wakes up, and he's a grown man sitting in a circle of defeated men who have nothing better to do than whine, complain, and bemoan circumstances they think they can't control—and probably don't even want to control.

Let's bring it close to home now, to you and your life. Our habits betray us. How easy is it to put off doing stuff we know we should do? You know the signs. Follow your gut. Listen to it or you will become a drifter, floating through life by circumstance. Drifting will make you comfortable in your misery.

Unless—

Unless something inside you snaps. Unless you are pissed off enough to just do it. If you're just going to complain and whine and drag others into your misery, you might as well be dead. Your existence would be ironically neutral, but at least it wouldn't be negative. Brutal much? Yep.

The whining all around me on the workroom floor was just annoying, a constant nagging, "You really should do that. You know what you need to do. This is something you ought to take care of sooner or later." But what did I do? I numbed the noise with my headphones. How often do we distract ourselves with this or that shiny thing when we know what we should be doing? Then when that gets old, we join in the complaining! It is easier to just laugh along and take the hit. Exactly what I did.

But then I got pissed. Super pissed. The grand circle of complainers became my mirror, and I saw who I was becoming. Heck, I heard it, too. "My future." Really? Why? Maybe it was up to that moment, but nothing changed until I did. That first step was about me, a statement of who I had chosen to be. The goal wasn't to make a scene and awesomely ride into the sunset like a heroic marauder (though that does sound pretty cool).

The point is, if you just wish you could take the leap, whatever it is—ask out the hottie from the coffee shop, finally enroll in the master's program, start that micro-business on the side, lose thirty pounds—then you can only get there when you take that first step off the cliff. Go with your gut, that voice deep inside that says, "Quit being a wimp, you already know what to do. There's nothing left to learn, figure out, or think about." The mind is where most battles are lost, so don't be too rational, or you'll create an excuse for yourself every single time.

Yeah, I'd decided to say something to the boss. But I didn't talk about doing it. I put myself right in the bullseye—smack dab in front of the boss man's desk. At that point, there literally was no going back. And that's when the magic happened. So it is when you take that first step off the scary cliff. Only once you're falling do you realize you've been wearing a parachute the whole time.

Let me give you the simplest framework. When you're facing a choice with multiple options, ask yourself, "Which choice will take me in the right direction?" It's very simple. No delays, no juggling of options. Make a decision.

Right now.

When I was surrounded by glum co-workers and a feeble boss, I could have bounced from one foot to the next, hoping things would turn around. Maybe I could drop a hint to the boss or try to just weather the storm?

But the longer I waited, the harder it was to take action.

So I didn't wait.

I knew where indecisiveness would lead me. Staying on that road meant my future would suck in 15 years.

In a split second, I dove right into the storm.

I took off to the boss' office that same second—the longer you try to ride motivation, the quicker it vanishes. So, I moved fast in my chosen direction.

In my humble experience, the key to good decision-making is confident decisiveness, which necessitates a certain measure of speed.

Now double down on your current life situations.

What are you chasing right now? Are you an aspiring engineer but hate math? In the context of career choices, are you making decisions based on what seems right or what you know in your heart?

Will that decision matter in a million years? Does your decision alter the course of history? You know you're going to die, so why would you spend your life unhappy? You've got to determine who you are making decisions for. Parents? Friends? Society? A significant other? The point is not that pleasing others is bad, the point is that you need to question your own motives and your need.

It's time for you to write your own chapter and make action-taking your reality.

It would be generic to say, "Just get good at decision-making," if there were no context to that decision-making.

So, here's what we'll do. Think about your life. Your career. Your relationships. Your hobbies. Your health.

Are you totally, completely, beyond-the-shadow-of-any-doubt satisfied with each of these?

If not, that's okay—simply because you now have the opportunity to make a life-changing decision for the better.

To move forward. To make progress. And the cool thing is, you aren't going to have to rely on your own ideas, creativity, or gut instinct to make that decision.

When I approached my boss, I went in already inspired by the story of people who had made a tough decision in a situation similar to the one I faced.

Same goes for you. Find someone who has conquered the area of life you are currently struggling with. It could be a famous person, an author, or somebody who is simply further along than you are.

Talk to them, listen to them. If the role model you want is inaccessible, read their books, articles, and blogs, or watch their videos. Simply make the decision to examine the past successful decisions of others that are worth emulating.

No guesswork needed here. Taking action starts with finding out what successful actions have already been taken by people you want to become like. It really is that easy.

So go make your decision.

WRITE YOUR OWN CHAPTER

Area of life you are facing big decisions in:

_____

_____

_____

_____

_____

A person who has done very well in that same area of life:

_____

_____

What decisions did this role model make in order to get where they wanted to be:

_____

_____

_____

_____

_____

A decision you will make based on what has worked (or hasn't) for other people facing a situation like yours:

_____
_____
_____
_____
_____
_____
_____
_____
_____
_____

START WITH GOOD ENOUGH

"There's no way this would pass inspection. I can spot like three dozen building code and safety violations right here. OSHA would love this," I said.

During my trip to Guatemala in 2011, I saw a five-story hospital being built. Sounds normal, right? A hospital's a hospital. Well, not when you're three hours from the nearest civilized town on the side of a mountain in the deep jungle. If you'd depend on a Lowes or Home Depot to get the job done, you're gonna have a tough time.

So, I watched as these construction

workers—all of whom probably had zero formal training, all trial and error experience—used what they had readily available to build this thing.

Branches cut straight from a tree to keep each floor from collapsing into the one just below it, that's what they stuffed between each floor supporting the next until the concrete dried.

Branches. Seriously. Perhaps the most surprising thing about all this? It worked. They stuffed so much between each floor that I bet it just so happened to meet or even surpass basic engineering integrity standards. They just did so in an unconventional—and sketchy-looking—way.

The construction team didn't have the right timing, situation, or circumstances. All they had was a need (to help the sick) and a goal (to fill that need by building a hospital). They could have complained that they didn't have the money, the connections, the influence, whatever.

But they just started where they were at and took the next step that was right in front of them. They didn't let the difficulty stop them, and they didn't focus on what they couldn't do.

Do you stop yourself before you start by focusing on the "large" steps? Or on what you can't do "now"? We use every excuse in the book it seems like to keep from doing hard things, even if what lies on the other side of the challenge is the fulfillment of our dream.

Like the Guatemalan builders, all you have to do is start where you're at. Here's an example of a guy who did just that—myself.

Again, do you need my stories? Not necessarily. But what example would I be setting if I didn't personally experience the challenge?

A challenge it was, kids. When I was breaking into the job market, I looked at careers that seemed I would be totally unqualified for. Did I let that stop me from looking into them?

No. Why would it? I had general construction training, but not museum-level or premium exhibit-caliber work experience. Yet.

So I went to the first company I could find and, instead of blindly shooting off my resume and whispering a prayer, and I asked the manager a question.

"What do I have to do to work here?"

I was 17 ½ at the time, so they couldn't legally hire me for a few more months.

They didn't ignore me or push me away. Instead, they explained almost everything I had to know in order to become a master carpenter for them. They outlined the duties, responsibilities, knowledge basis…everything! They basically told me to learn all of that stuff, then when I turned 18, they'd have a serious conversation about bringing me onboard.

I spent the next few months studying what I would be doing and preparing myself to work at the same level as those with 30+ years' experience—and get paid the salary of someone who was by no means a rookie.

It worked; they brought me aboard just weeks after my birthday, and I spent the next 5 years there. That position was the crucial stepping stone to the career I have now, where I'm consistently earning 2x, even 3x, what other people my age are at their jobs—all because I went for something I "wasn't ready for."

So, what's your why? I was hungry for a career that wasn't mundane, tedious, or meaningless, which is why I went after something I wasn't qualified for. That was my why.

What is something—a cause, a project, an idea—that has been on the back-burner for awhile? Maybe you haven't had the money or time. Or maybe it's just possible that you have more excuses than resources.

Here's an example; maybe your cause is to clean up all your city's waterways, rivers, and streams. Quite a tall order that is, even in the smallest country town. So jump on what's right in front of you—the first mile of the first river that's closest to you. Gather up some friends or co-workers, and spend every other weekend on beautifying that first mile.

That's a start, and a start is all you need.

As another example, you may want to get into good shape. You want to get ripped, have that six-pack, and brag about a 48-inch vertical leap. Don't go all crazy and buy a thousand dollars' worth of protein shakes or hire a personal trainer for $200/hour. Instead, run just 1 mile every other day. Or jog. Heck, a walk would be good enough! Just start.

And that right there is the key—good enough. Start out just good enough to build momentum little by little. The more progress you make—and the more consistently you make it—the fewer excuses you'll have in your repertoire.

Just look at what's right in front of you, take what you've got, and jump on your cause.

Start now. What sticks can you find in the forest to keep your hospital from collapsing into itself?

You've got two hands to carry tools and two feet to get you there. Now go and forage.

WRITE YOUR OWN CHAPTER

Your "why":

_____

_____

_____

_____

_____

Ideas, resources, tools, and relationships you have right now to start with:

_____

_____

_____

Record progress below. What you got done today to move closer to the goal:

_____

_____

_____

_____

_____

THE STYROFOAM ELEPHANT IN THE ROOM

When Michelangelo sculpted David, he claimed that when he started with a giant block of marble, all he needed to do was chisel away everything from the marble block that wasn't the likeness of David.

The same is true with the elephant in the room.

No, not the cliché. Literally, the elephant in the room. The one made from foam, steel, pipes, and paint. With a chainsaw.

When I launched into my career as an exhibit carpenter, my first job required me to work on a project for a waterpark in Denver, Colorado. The exact assignment—sculpt a water feature that sprayed visitors from the trunks of two life-sized elephants.

So where do you start on a project like this?

Our imaginations. As soon as my team was awarded the project, we downloaded as many pictures of elephants we could possibly get our hands on.

We made sketches. Took photos of photos. Played around with their appearance in Photoshop. With clear shots of every angle of the beast, we impressed into our minds the exact image of what we were assigned to create.

That creative spark we felt drove us to productivity. First the steel frames. Then the water pipes set in place within the plastic and foam body. Finally, cutting away corners and rough edges using hot wire knives and chainsaws.

At every turn, we referred back to the images of the elephants we gathered. With what we gathered in our research, we might as well have built ourselves a real, live elephant.

Once we'd transformed the mix of materials into a reasonable facsimile of an elephant's body, we brought in a group of local artists to take on the fine detailing, such as facial expressions, skin folds, shadows, tusks, and toes. They likewise used a binder of photos as their map.

From initial creative spark to functioning trunk-spraying elephants, a mere eight weeks had passed.

Anything we create in reality has first been created in our imaginations. This mental world is just as real as the physical one, if not more so since it is the source. If we hadn't first imagined what the elephant statues looked like, there would have been no creating it. No mental blueprint, no physical structure as the result.

The process had its up's and down's, fun parts and not-so-fun parts. Nonetheless, we reached the end and achieved our goal because we started right—with a mental blueprint.

Our designer looked at hundreds and

hundreds of pictures of elephants—multiple breeds, ages, colors, and sizes. With an outcome so intensely visualized, the result could not possibly have been anything else.

With the image in mind our focus shifted to that next cut, that next brushstroke, that next chip away at what wasn't part of the elephant's likeness.

And we didn't think small either. Unlike some who pursue microscopic versions of their goals because it's "more practical" or "realistic," we pursued life-sized, lifelike creations. Have you ever seen a fully matured elephant in the wild? No? Well, if you ever go to a certain waterpark in Denver, Colorado, you'll see replicas of ones.

Since you're still reading at this point, I gather that there's a goal, dream, ambition, or desire you've got on simmer. There's a host of good ideas floating around in your head, but you haven't made the first cut yet. Let's change that.

If you're ready to change, keep reading. If you're not ready to change, keep reading.

Take your goal. The dream. That

ambition. Your desire. It's time to build a blueprint, starting with what you have—or even what you don't.

As with the elephant, figure out what materials you need. Want to launch into freelance graphic design on the side? Then are you gonna need a website? A portfolio featuring your best work to date?

Have a dream to play guitar in your church's music group? Figure out what the three or four songs are they play most often, hit up the internet to find out what chords make up those songs, and practice, practice, practice.

Whatever your goal, ask yourself BS-blasting questions. How much time do you actually need? Don't under-guess. What are your deadlines? Don't make them up, or convenient excuses will allow you to procrastinate. What metrics do you need to hit to consistently get where you want to be?

Here's a solid example of that last one, the most important question of all. Let's say you want to clean up our planet, like the folks over at The Ocean Cleanup.

A 19 year-old kid came up with the idea of removing all the plastic and trash from the Pacific Ocean by leveraging the ocean's own currents.

And it works! Now, I'm sure a lot of folks thought his very, very big goal was crazy, reckless, or impossible. One kid taking on years of industrial and consumer pollution? Yeah, right.

But, he stuck to his vision, put his team together, and now—he's cleaning up the ocean.

The kid knew what his "elephant" was going to look like, so he fashioned each shape of his "Styrofoam" plan to match what he saw in his mind.

Like this kid here, you can make an utterly audacious goal come to pass simply by taking a very small first step. That's all you have to do. As long as you keep in mind your target—what your completed "elephant" will look like—throw yourself into the details of each step in your plan.

While my end goal was two elephant statues, my focus was that very next half-inch cut across its body.

The Ocean Cleanup kid's end goal was to make our planet, starting with our oceans, a cleaner place. But his next step was designing the right kind of net to help the ocean self-filter its own currents.

Your end goal is to finish this book without quitting or getting your tears all over the pages of my book (don't you dare). But your next step is to write down your goal's blueprint and the accompanying metrics.

Then the elephant in the room won't be the fact you've put this goal-achieving business off for so long. You're welcome.

WRITE YOUR OWN CHAPTER

Your next goal:

_____

_____

_____

The next step today:

_____

_____

_____

_____

How that next step got you closer to the goal:

_____

_____

_____

_____

_____

FACING THE BITE

Everything is possible. But it's gonna take more guts than you think you have right now. Face that bite.

"AAAAHHHHHHHHHHH!!!!" my little brother's ten-second scream of terror.

I tossed my action figures onto the table and made my way to the back porch of my aunt's house. Since the backyard sloped down a hill about a hundred yards, I couldn't see my brother or the source of his terror.

With the naïve courage of my seven years on this planet, I took off across the lawn and scurried down the hill.

Two figures. My dad. My brother. My dad carrying my brother. My kicking and screaming brother.

And a third.

My aunt's dog tied to a cable. An Alaskan Malamute. A cross between a wolf and a husky. Basically a Yeti when you're my age.

The giant mass of fur licked my brother's feet, like any supposedly friendly dog does. Barry, my brother, didn't quite get this. I preferred to keep my distance, too. So now that I could see Barry's screams were unwarranted and the dog was restrained, I turned around to return to the house.

Snap

The cable broke. I saw Dingo bare his teeth through a growl and latch itself onto Barry's tiny leg.

Dad wrestled Barry away and rushed him into the house. I then did what any kid my age would've done—but never should have.

I ran as fast as my light-up shoes would take me.

No more than five seconds later, the dog ripped into my hip, but I felt nothing. I had definitely passed out. The first bite ripped four inches of flesh off of my leg. As my dad ran back out to me, "Dingo" sank his teeth into my shoulder and began to drag me towards the cornfield…

Thirteen stiches for Barry and thirty-one for me later, I found myself a new owner of a condition called Cynophobia—the fear of dogs.

Every dog's bark made me cringe. When every boy your age can't wait to play with the neighbor's dog come summer time, yet you're busy writing out a list of watertight excuses as to why you can't join your friends because you know you're gonna have a bad time.

By age fifteen, I'd come to the realization that hiding behind my parents whenever I see a dog isn't the most attractive thing to the ladies.

So you know what I did? I decided to stop being scared of dogs. Yes, that's right. Anyone reading this whose ever experienced a phobia before knows it is easier said than done.

Or is it?

Just do what you're scared of.

I didn't have long to wait.

Not long after my sixteenth birthday, I enjoyed a parent-free weekend with my brother and two buddies from school. Around midnight, we set up shop on the back porch to shoot the breeze, build a campfire in the backyard, and drink Red Bull.

Not even ten minutes into our night, Danny (my youngest brother) spotted a pack of coyotes.

Two…Four…Six…Eight…

I counted the reflecting yellow eyes in pairs. Every few seconds the eyes got bigger.

"They're coming for our dog," whispered Barry.

"Let's chase them!" I said. "Who's in?"

We made our way to the tool shed adjacent to the house, and I kicked the door open like a boss.

Baseball bat, a walking stick, a tennis racket, and grandpa's wooden cane. We promptly armed ourselves.

No time for a pep talk, we were ready for battle.

We stood mid-yard staring into the field

in the direction we last saw them. Weapons high, voices peaked, we yelled and charged at them running them all off into the darkness.

Since the coyote confrontation that night, I have never felt scared of a dog.

Easier said than done? Sometimes yes. And sometimes no.

Seven years later, I was on a morning jog at the metro park near my house. These go-around's are usually pretty quiet. But on this one, two girls with a leashed boxer faced me as I rounded a corner.

I didn't change directions. I didn't look away. I didn't head to the other side of the trail.

I just stared her down.

The dog, not the girls.

As soon as I reached the girls, I bent down and reached my hand out to the dog. They say you're supposed to put out your fist to a dog you don't know, but I held my open palm out there for the pooch. Instantly, his conniption fit ceased, and I scratched his chin. (*Disclaimer*—I can't guarantee you won't get bit if you try this.)

"Wow, he's never let anyone pet him before like that," one of the girls said. "At least not without barking like crazy."

In fighting what looked like a losing battle against my fear of dogs, I finally won the war by unknowingly following the old adage, "Act as if, so then it shall be."

That's exactly what my brothers and I and my buddies did that cold evening several years ago. We faced the bite by acting like we weren't scared.

That time in the park, I gave all the signs that I was bigger than my fear, I was greater than that boxer. And so it responded to me as I directed it to. Act as if, so then it shall be.

Looking back, I remember how much I hated being scared. It took me nine years to hate the idea of being afraid more than I was afraid.

So. What are the big dogs in your life?

When I was a kid, I busied myself with lists of excuses so I wouldn't need to face my fears. At least I could cope with my phobia, right? At least I had some kind of pacifier to keep myself calm, right?

What are you replacing your fears with?

As a young kid, I always found excuses not to be around dogs (i.e., only hanging out with friends that *didn't* have dogs).

But when my fear faced me, I faced it right back. I faced the bite. I couldn't distract myself from fear any longer. And because I didn't run towards an excuse, I didn't need one anymore. No longer would I miss out on fun with friends or good stories just because I was scared.

Ask yourself what would happen if you don't do the thing you're scared of. Go deep with the answer. Think of other aspects of your life (unrelated to the fear) that may be affected by this fear. Your confidence will be boosted and doors will open to you that you didn't see while masked with fear.

Time to write your own chapter. With the following action steps, you will effectively conquer fear once and for all.

WRITE YOUR OWN CHAPTER

Your Big Fear:

_____

_____

_____

_____

Things you can do to avoid facing it:

_____

_____

_____

_____

_____

What happens if fear wins:

_____

_____

_____

_____

_____

How you will defeat fear:

LOST, YET KNOWING EXACTLY WHERE YOU ARE

"So Nathan," my project manager took off his glasses, "how would you like to travel? An assignment's come up for us. It'll be about a year, and the location's over six hundred miles away. Sound like fun?"

What ambitious eighteen year-old professional with rugged confidence would say no to an offer like this? To travel hundreds of miles into the concrete jungle of New York City, put my particular set of skills to use, and be paid handsomely for a career adventure unlike any other—it was the dream of every young man with entrepreneurial drive.

That's all cool. At least, it would be cool. If it were true.

In reality, I was a scrawny kid with an under-developed ego and a just-earned high school diploma. I'd spent my entire life in the two-stoplight town of Arcanum, Ohio, and my grandest adventure to date was a brief trip to Florida.

To the beach.

With my family.

When I was seven.

Imagine this culture shock to eighteen year-old me.

So I did what anyone with my background and experience (or lack thereof) in my shoes would do. I swallowed hard and said, "Sure."

Time to grow up, Nathan.

That I did. Every evening after work, night after night, month after month, I roamed the city streets.

From Times Square's intersection of

media to Soho's hundred-year old abandoned alleys to the towering structures of the Financial District.

No sense of time, no sense of direction. Lost in my own curiosity, I found my imagination. Lost on location, yet I knew exactly where I was.

Completely in the moment. Present in my surroundings. Exploring until bedtime.

In this photo, there is a story of exploration to revelation.

The dark, dingy, abandoned, flooded hull of the USS Intrepid, a retired aircraft carrier turned military museum my employer was hired to renovate.

On the USS Intrepid are nine floors—nine floors. Only four of them are above water. So what kind of hidden memories lie down deep, I wondered.

I peeked down the hatch during my lunch break one afternoon several months into the job. One…two…three…four… I could count each floor from my vantage point as my gaze descended into darkness.

Onto the rusted-out ladder my hands

went. The rest of me followed.

Musty. Freezing. Moist.

Curiosity—and scary fascination—carried me deeper into the darkness. I crawled my way into a tiny hallway, made my way through a series of doors, and came across a second series of ladders that ushered me into the bowels of the Intrepid's hull.

By the time I reached my third or fourth locked door and immovable hatch, the thought struck me—How do I get out of here?

An hour's worth of fumbling backwards through nearly six hundred feet of darkness later, I emerged from the iron labyrinth on the hangar deck at the other end of the ship.

In this chilling experience, I've learned…

Everywhere leads to somewhere.

In this case, I mean physically, but the principle applies to life choices as well.

There was no wrong turn for me, for instance. And there is no wrong decision for you. There is the choice you make, and the consequences that come with it. If you made a choice that your mind colors as "bad," you're going to waste energy and effort regretting it. This is energy and effort, mind you, that could have been spent rectifying the situation.

It's okay to wonder, and it's okay to explore—in life as in ships—but do yourself a favor and don't judge things as good or bad.

What the mind labels as bad is merely another route. This route may lead you somewhere better than your original destination, or it might teach you a lesson. Either way, take it and learn.

Looking back, this elementary reflection stemmed from both my treks through Manhattan and my trip through the Intrepid's darkest corridors. Maybe that sentence about not making a judgment is simplistic, but in it is a world of philosophy.

When physical curiosity takes you beyond the point of no return, you can find previously uncovered strengths. You've probably heard the saying, "Not all who wander are lost." In my case, wandering got me lost in the greatest find of my life—discovering the self-reliance of my young adult self.

You see, we all want to find our true

selves. But I've found it helps if you get lost somewhere uncomfortable first. You may start to panic or get awkward, but you mustn't run from the situation, or you'll in reality be running from yourself. Here you can meet yourself in the darkness, in the aloneness.

It's the awkward, dirty, and downright scary times of life that draw out your real self. When you persevere through even the slightly uncomfortable seasons, you emerge on the other side stronger—and even more fulfilled—than ever.

Your true, fulfilled self is defined by your experiences, and when you persevere through the tough experiences, you find you're a lot tougher than you thought.

Sounds blindingly obvious, I know. How is this idea of perseverance even actionable? Think about the gym for a moment. We go there to shred our muscle fibers, wear down our energy, and push our lungs to the limit. If that's how fitness centers advertised, only gluttons for punishment would buy memberships. But what the workout faithful know is that on the other side of all that wear and tear on their bodies is improved health, increased energy, sexier appearance, and skyrocketed confidence.

So it is with life. Our ego can get shredded. Our joys can be crushed. Our emotions are sent through the ringer. But just like resting from weightlifting, healing from life's bruises repairs our strength—and makes us even greater than we were before.

This is what I mean by perseverance. You may not be able to affect the immediate situation to the extent you'd like, but if you change your outlook, you can change your outcome in the long-run.

So, what kind of person do you want to become through the trials you invariably will face? I recommend deciding ahead of time.
When you become that person—your true self—what will you think about every day? What will you daydream about? What type of friends do you want to have? How is your personality even more authentic to the type of person you've always wanted to be?

This isn't about hitting deadlines or completing goals, it's about mastering the core of who you are by focusing on and designing your life.

Now it's time to write your own chapter. When covering topics like finding yourself through perseverance, there's a tendency to swing to the extreme of life coach-esque fluff. I'm not into that. When you fall, get up. When quitting crosses your mind, remember the people you are doing it for, and fight on. Tough times are only temporary, but tough people will last.

It's easy to talk about life hacks, mental barriers to overcome, and high performance topics. In fact, there are entire industries built around telling you, "You are worth it!" and other inspirations that get you excited but don't push you to take action. It's much more uncomfortable to talk about hard-core preparation for the tough times in life, the grungy places within the rusty hull where up is down and down is up.

Here's what I want you to do. Think about your situation. Yes, that one. We all have one. You try not to think about it too much, but your untrained mind can't escape it.

Write down what type of person you have to be to get through your situation on top—mentally, emotionally, physically.

The person you want to be should be so great that the task at hand will appear to be insignificant. Then, pick up the hammer, or make the phone call. Whatever it is, jump at the task head-first. Get stronger.

The good news? You will know without a single doubt that when life gets tough, you are even tougher.

WRITE YOUR OWN CHAPTER

"A problem well-stated is a problem half-solved."
~ Charles Kettering

Your problem well-stated:

_____

_____

_____

What your life looks like when the problem is solved for good:

_____

_____

_____

To make this happen, who do you want to become mentally:

_____

_____

_____

_____

To make this happen, who do you want to become emotionally:

___

___

___

___

___

To make this happen, who do you want to become physically:

___

___

___

___

___

GET OFF THE SIDELINES

The young man made his way across the dance floor towards his beloved. As friends and family of all ages shuffled around him, he reached his hand out.

No words were needed.

His wife took him by the hand, and off they went.

They waltzed their way to the center of the dance floor, parting the crowd around them. Whistling and clapping cheered them on.

My best friend Brent and his wife Astrid, dancing away the night at his older brother's wedding. But there I stood on the sidelines, sipping punch that had too little alcohol.

I took a few more steps away from the dance floor, thinking of more excuses not to participate.

Then it hit me.

Nobody cared.

Nobody cared if I looked like an idiot. If I toppled over trying to spin around. If I was totally out of rhythm.

Nobody cared.

Standing there with one hand in my pocket and one hand bearing a Styrofoam cup, I did kinda look like an idiot. A drag.

So what if somebody took a video of me on their cell, titled it "white kid sucks at dancing," and had it go viral on YouTube?

So I danced.

It was a memorable night.

You see, it doesn't matter what you look like when you just get out there and dance, because you'll still look like more of a fun person than the kid twiddling his thumbs by the punch bowl.

From now on, dance—whenever possible

as often as possible. Whatever your version of dancing—be it gardening, playing basketball, improv classes, whatever—just keep dancing! Feel young, stay alive. Troubles vanish in the moment. Create memories. Unleash laughter. Need more reasons to dance? You can defeat shyness, make new friends, burn calories, and build self-confidence.

Now go dance!

You're welcome.

Just watching others have fun, laugh, and succeed is nowhere close to the level of enjoyment of actually jumping in yourself. Get off the sidelines!

Let's get real here for a moment. What do you want your life to look like? By that, I mean—what "dances" are you watching other people do? What games are you watching other people play?

Not gonna lie, it's easier to watch sports on TV or listen to the podcast guru on building a business than it is to put in the training to be that guy out there on the field everyone's watching or the entrepreneur who lands yet another high-profile deal. But is that what you really want, to go through life as an observer? Is it worth it to be above mediocrity?

It's not like you have to be "the best" either, whatever that means. In the 2014 World Cup, some German kid kicked the game-winning goal, and he was immediately hailed as a national hero. But if he were a perfect soccer player, Germany wouldn't have needed overtime to win the match.

Trying your best is what's important. That's what the German kid did. All he had to be was good enough to kick the ball so that it was just a couple of inches out of the goalkeeper's reach.

Think about that—whatever game you're trying to win, all you have to do is be a couple of inches worth better than your opponent. Can you do that?

By this point, I know at least a handful of readers are thinking, "Yeah, Nathan, I get it. But see, I love watching college basketball, I just hate playing it."

To that I ask, why? How did that come to be? When did someone else tell you that you sucked at it? Give a kid a hoop and a ball, and he'll have the time of his life. But give that same kid a hoop, a ball, and a bunch of other kids watching, and there's a fair chance his confidence will be crushed after only a couple of air balls. Now you look back on this like it's funny, or it's just the way it is.

Let me ask you this. Would you rather watch somebody behind the wheel of the sports car of your dreams, or would you rather drive it yourself?

Duh.

Therefore, why would you rather watch the couple dance, see the German kid kick the game-winning goal, and watch college basketball? What's stopping you from having your own personal World Cup-winning goal to kick?

Getting into the game can be easy. Enjoy cheering for your favorite NFL team every Sunday? Go try out for flag football at your local YMCA or other community rec center.

Stay up to an ungodly hour on weekends playing city-building strategy video games? Find out when your city's developers and construction masterminds are having meetings open to the community, and go.

Does your iPod overflow with tunes from The Beatles? Pick a local Karaoke bar and sing a song or two of theirs. Everybody will be drunk anyway, so no need to worry about embarrassing yourself.

Write your own chapter. Make an appointment for and with yourself. What have you sidelined yourself from? It's time to leave the punch bowl behind and go find a hot girl to dance with.

WRITE YOUR OWN CHAPTER

What potentially exciting activity you could be really good at that you've sidelined yourself from:

_____

_____

_____

Where people go to enjoy that activity near where you live:

_____

_____

_____

_____

How you put yourself in the middle of it:

_____

_____

_____

_____

_____

What you learned about yourself by "getting off the sidelines":

_____
_____
_____
_____
_____
_____
_____
_____
_____
_____

NATHAN KESSLER

KARMA'S ADVANTAGE

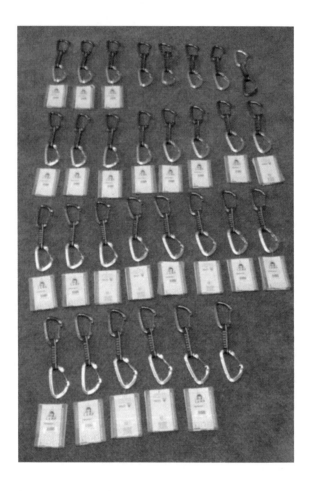

My brothers and I stood staring at each other. Then back at the open package we'd just received in the mail. Then back at each other. Then back at the package.

"So, what should we do with these?"

Barry scratched the back of his head.

"Sweeeeet." I ran my fingers over our unexpected prize.

Inside the package lay thirty quick draws used for rock climbing, a hobby of ours.

But we'd bought only five. Yet here were thirty. These things aren't cheap. Three hundred bucks worth of quick draws for only sixty dollars.

"What should we do?" Barry asked again.

"It feels like Christmas morning," I said, imagining these tools with me as I scaled the face of the next slab of rock we were going to tackle.

"Yeah, it does." Barry nodded. "Somebody screwed up big time at the warehouse."

"They sure did. I wonder if they'll lose their job." I looked again at the five-item order sheet nestled into the package next to the quick draws.

"Hope not." Barry's voice lost its 'Christmas morning tone.' "Just think, we'll be hundreds of feet above the ground with these possibly cursed things."

"Quick draws we didn't pay for." Barry muttered.

"...that may cost some family their sole source of income, or at least a big piece of their paycheck." I finished.

Barry and I looked at each other. Then back at the package. And back at each other one last time.

"Let's send them back," we said together.

Neither of us said it, but I could tell we were both thinking it—Karma is a cruel, cruel mistress. Don't screw with her.

Sure, we could have kept quiet about the mistake, and nothing bad would have happened. To us, at least. Regardless, somebody was probably going to be written up and have about $240 deducted from his pay.

You don't fool with the laws of the universe, especially when someone else's livelihood is at stake. And possibly even your own life. We all know right from wrong. Always do right.

I'm sure some people reading this think Karma's a joke. To those uneducated in her ways, I say: give your nasty deed a few years. What goes around comes around.

Several years ago, I was in the process of closing on my second property at 24 years old. It would have instantly given me equity—to the tune of $72,000…at 24. But when I prepared to finalize the mortgage I'd need to do so, a discrepancy planted itself firmly in my path—the pay stubs from my job didn't match my W2 from that year. Thus, the underwriter refused to sign off on the loan I'd nearly gotten approval for. Somebody in charge of payroll couldn't do basic math.

Naturally, I took it up with the big man in charge at work. All he had to do was write a letter to the loan company stating the simple reason for the discrepancy—his company made a mistake—and all would be well.

Nope. He sent a letter to the loan company. Two, actually. Both letters had the answers to everything except the question being asked—why is there a discrepancy? As a result, I received a "Terminated Contract" email that made my fists clench—and the deal vanish.

"Because you have not been able to obtain financing, the contract has been terminated."

As soon as $72k slipped through my fingers, the owner of the company I worked for came begging, saying he would do whatever it took to make things right. A significant raise? A new position?

"Now you care! All you had to do was answer one simple question. One tiny, simple, ridiculously straightforward question. And you blew it for me."

What followed was a "mistakes were made" speech that shifted the blame to everyone but him and his company.

I gave my one week's notice that afternoon. Getting $72k ripped out of your hands because an employer I trusted couldn't keep his numbers straight isn't an experience that just goes away with time. Several months after I quit, still fuming, I marched myself into his office to demand what was rightfully mine.

Defensive and standoffish, he responded, "You have to understand, Nathan, I have the facts on my side. My team will stand by me."

So glad I didn't have to deal with this guy anymore. New job, less stress, better pay. Too bad it took me $72k to get me out of here.

"You didn't care about me at all. You were just covering yourself because you screwed up." I got serious.

"Well, you know what, I know how you feel." My old boss crossed his arms. Oh, do you? "Yesterday, we had a seven million dollar deal in our back pocket. The returning client had told us for over a year that this project was ours. Just yesterday, they flew in from Virginia yesterday to check out our facilities. They told us we were their first choice. Then last night just before midnight, they awarded the contract to our top competitor," he said in a shaky voice. I could tell that the shock kept his voice and his head low.

By the end of this heated meeting, I forgave him. I stopped all legal actions against him, and let it be. Karma caught up to him.

No matter how sorry this guy said he was, no apology was going to fill my bank account. So many lessons I could extract from this event—from greed and human nature to forgiveness and responsibility. And of course, Karma.

How's Karma at work in your life? You've probably never done someone dirty for tens of thousands of dollars (or maybe you have), but I want this story to inspire you to get up and put some positive actions in your bank of Karma.

To start small and prove this works, let's do this. Hold the door open for someone else. When you do, you'll soon find people holding the door open for you. It's that simple.

Now, it's time to write your own chapter.

More specifically, I want to throw down this challenge—find three random strangers today. Notice something unique or cool about each of them. Walk up to them out of the blue, and pay them that compliment.

Seriously. Do it. Three strangers, three compliments, three dollars into Karma's bank (or whatever they're worth).

As you see Karma operate in the small ways in your life, you'll recognize it in major ways in other areas.

WRITE YOUR OWN CHAPTER

The unique characteristic of each person you encountered and complimented:

_____

_____

_____

_____

_____

How did you feel doing something that you didn't expect anything in return for:

_____

_____

_____

_____

_____

_____

_____

_____

IMPROVISE!

"Ah, s***," I muttered. "No way this is happening. Have to start all over."

During my museum exhibit construction days, We built a life-sized replica space shuttle. Quite the task, so of course there were going to be problems.

The first one?

A one-eighth of an inch problem.

We were supposed to line up the wooden doors I'd fabricated over the steel beams some other company had fabricated, then bolt them together. Because the holes were drilled by a machinist and the doors built by a carpenter, I knew there had to be leeway in case there was even in a miniscule misalignment because there were 96 holes.

Doesn't take a genius to realize that a carpenter is *not* going to match the tolerances of a machinist. The machinists' spacing was accurate down to $1/1000^{th}$ of an inch, but our accuracy was to only $1/16^{th}$, a $1/32^{nd}$ maybe.

I knew this would happen, and I even warned them ahead of time. But nope, our company's draftsmen went according to plan—and promptly delayed the project schedule.

We wasted 7 days, 3 drills, and dozens of drill bits starting all over, using our own drills to make larger holes in the metal beams so they'd be in direct alignment with the wooden door brackets.

Oh, and did I mention that this project took place during the we-don't-have-any-money-to-pay-you-guys phase of the job.

Life rarely goes according to plan. The more prepared you are for things to not go according to plan, the better off your results will be. We were a little pissed they didn't listen to us, but instead of yelling at the knuckleheads in charge, we embraced the grind and worked it out. Most of the time, improvised solutions require sweat equity.

Being prepared to improvise is an acquired skill, I believe—not necessarily something that comes natural. But it's not difficult to learn when you open your mind to a host of obvious-though-unplanned alternatives.

When you paddle a canoe down a river, you have to go with the flow. Rarely do you ever take a "straight" path. If you obsess over following a linear plan whilst canoeing, soon you'll find yourself stuck trying to paddle up a riverbank.

So be flexible, and keep going toward where you know you want to be, not necessarily where "the plan" says you're supposed to go during that process.

Take flight plans, for instance. Airliners rarely if ever fly in a straight direction toward their destinations. They plan according to reality—other airplanes, storms, wind, etc. They plan for improvisations long before they ever have to make them.

Be careful about this contingency planning idea though. I don't want you running through all the potential disasters you might happen upon on the way to accomplishing your dream or goal only to let fear stop you.

Yes, if you're building something, bring extra tools. If you're starting a business, have cash reserves on hand to cushion your career transition. But don't negatively color future events by obsessing over what could go wrong. People who live to avoid the worst case scenarios never get to enjoy the best case scenarios.

You know, nowadays the conventional wisdom is to plan, plan, plan...prepare, prepare, prepare. Casting your vision ahead of time is important, don't get me wrong. I certainly had the skills and tools necessary to tackle the shuttle design project long before showing up for work.

But don't forget about reaction, improvising. When a bump comes, don't get stuck going back to the drawing board by default. And if you have time constraints, you don't have time to waste re-planning and re-preparing. Master the skill of improvisation, and you won't confuse following a plan with reaching your goal.

If you know your direction is wrong, don't get cocky and stick it out just because it's yours. Stay focused, but be flexible on the way.

Alright kids, I'm letting you off the hook today. No immediate action steps. Improvising is not something you can practice ahead of time. Be AWARE of reacting. When the time comes, you'll know what to do.

WRITE YOUR OWN CHAPTER

In what situations did you find yourself having to improvise recently:

_____

_____

_____

_____

_____

_____

_____

_____

_____

_____

_____

_____

_____

FORTY THOUSAND DOLLARS? OR FORTY BUCKS?

The speaker bounded his way up the stage, snapped his wireless head mic in place, and waved to the crowd.

A crowd of seventeen people.

"With what you're about to learn tonight, I can all but guarantee you will be earning ten, twenty, even fifty thousand in virtually ninety days or less." The dude pointed right at me in the front row. "Here's the kicker. You can do it all with no money down!"

At twenty years old, you think I would

have known better. Then again, at twenty years old, you want a far-flung promise like that to be true.

The DJ played some cheesy synthesizer tune that sounded like it was meant to symbolize 80's pop culture.

"Nearly no work, nearly no effort, nearly no time." The speaker peered over the audience. "All this can be yours!"

I saw dollar signs.

Literally, I saw dollar signs.

The next PowerPoint slide flashed onto the screen behind the speaker—a looping image of hundred dollar bills floating in place above a mansion with a front yard sign reading, "Foreclosed."

I can be an investor, a real investor! The thought hit me.

"And if you come back for our three-day session this weekend for an exclusive discount, we will show you exactly how to make this dream life, your life. Step by step, guaranteed! If you aren't overwhelmingly satisfied with everything you will learn in this weekend's session, we will award you access to next week's five-day workshop for half-off the price of tuition."

Looking back, I wish I could tell you that I shook my head, cursed the get-rich-quick scheme under my breath, and booked it out of there.

Nope.

I wrote a check before night's end to pay for the three-day session. $1,200. Then the week-long workshop the week after. $24,000 split between me and my investing partner. Next, a trip to the Vegas strip, followed by an inner circle coaching program. $15,000, also split. Wiping out savings and maxing out credit cards. A little over $40k between me and my investing partner.

I would like to report that after just four weeks of undergoing all this training, I bought and flipped my first property, earning a hefty check of about $75k that more than made up for the "investment" I'd made.

I would like to report that, anyway.

To say I was uncomfortable with my decision to pursue this training would be the understatement of my 20's. I had zero experience buying and selling houses. Sometimes there just are no shortcuts.

About six months later, we finally found a property within my budget. Looked pretty good on the outside, just some paint and landscaping. Inside needed several things, mainly for cosmetic purposes. Plus, it was handicap-accessible! Surely there was a market for such a niche place to live.

As soon as my business partner and I shook on our decision to buy the property, I rushed to the bank, got approved for a $62,000 loan, and began chasing what the speaker promised.

This tiny voice in the back of my head kept saying, "You just signed your life away."

I was able to shut out all this "negative self-talk"—that's what our inner circle coaching mentor told me these fears were—until bills and taxes flooded my mailbox.

The day I swung open the door of "my" home, I thought to myself, *"This will be so simple."*

It took EIGHTEEN months to prove me right. Eighteen grueling, sucky, open-house-filled months. We were just going to clean up the carpets, scrape out the gutters, and slap a new screen door on the back. But we ended up installing new carpets, gutting the kitchen, and slapping a new coat of paint on every wall and ceiling.

We ushered over 250 people through that place before finally selling it to an older woman who could appreciate and get plenty of use out of the handicap-accessible features. After the deal went through, I told myself, "I never want to go to Lowes again."

When the sale was final, I took a check straight to the bank and counted my return on investment—$10,000.

Maybe my dream of making millions as a no-money-down house-flipper wasn't quite realistic, but the idea of learning how to earn some cash on the side through responsibly purchasing, fixing up, and selling residential properties is, in my mind, still a worthy goal.

How often do we hear our friends, family, or colleagues talk about that crazy dream of theirs they've always wanted to go after? Maybe it was learning a new language.

Perhaps your buddy has always wanted to start a micro-business on the side. Or maybe simply trimming down to run a marathon.

Whatever your dream or goal, it's a lot easier to talk about what you want to get than it is to talk about *how* and *when* you'll get it done—and even harder to then actually do it!

When we attended the real estate investment gig, we were totally fired up with reasons why we were diving head-first into the house-flipping game. We simply assumed the program would tell us exactly what to do, like a recipe that would cook us up success every single time.

When that proved not to be the case, you bet we were pissed. But after forking over $40k, we realized only two options remained.

One, we could cut the losses. Better luck next time.

Two, we could look at the $40,000 as an investment in ourselves, as progress on our journey towards profit on our first property, and as self-accountability that forced us to continue—because we'd only come so far.

You're reading this right now because we

went with option number two.

The only reason we didn't give up when faced with the challenge of buying, fixing, and selling that first property was simple, now that I look back on the ordeal. The pain of giving up before following through on our dream of becoming house-flippers would be worse than the pain of jumping into the unknown realm of real estate.

As with all these stories, a beautiful lesson emerges. At the end of the day, did I need all of that training? No, but it served an invaluable purpose—I got some skin in the game in pursuit of my dream.

Now, I'm not suggesting you stretch your credit to hold yourself accountable to fulfilling your ambitions. But you do need to stretch your comfort zone.

I could have gotten all the real estate investing info from the workshops via Google or YouTube, but I didn't. What we paid $40,000 for wasn't the training, it was an investment in ourselves and our dream. People only value what they pay for. On an entrepreneurship podcast I listened to recently, I heard a story of this business coach who offered complementary consulting sessions to readers of his blog. But none of these casual students reached the dynamic levels of growth that his premium clients experienced. So as soon the non-paying students starting paying him for the coaching, they got serious about it and thus started seeing results.

Time for you to write your own chapter and put some skin in the game in the pursuit of your own dream! Here's one way to make yourself accountable to reaching the results you desire.

Consult two of your real, genuine, trustworthy friends, tell them both what your big idea/goal/ambition/dream/desire is, and guarantee to each of them that you will have that first small step completed by X date. And if you don't complete that first small step by then, you will give each of your friends $20. Or up the amount if $20 doesn't mean much to you.

Worst case scenario, you will have learned my $40,000 lesson for only $40.

So, how much action will you take? Where are you at in life right now? And do you want to stay there for the next year? Or more?

Your choice. If you've read this far, I know you've got what it takes to make the right one.

WRITE YOUR OWN CHAPTER

Your idea/goal/ambition/dream/desire:

_____

_____

_____

_____

_____

Two friends to consult:

_____

_____

Your first small step:

_____

_____

_____

_____

_____

_____

_____

Date to complete first small step by:

_____

_____

How'd it go? Good? Continue on. Bad? Start again:

_____

_____

_____

_____

_____

_____

_____

_____

_____

DO HARD THINGS

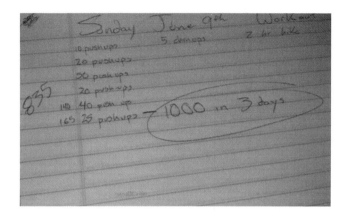

"1,000 pushups, man." My cousin shook his head. "That's intense."

I wasn't familiar with the specifics of his summer football practice routine, so I asked, "Are you talking like 1,000 pushups in one hour, in one day…I mean, what are we talking here?"

My cousin heaved a sigh of defeat. "They expect us to do 1,000 pushups in a single week."

I blinked twice. "Really? That's it?"

"That's it!?" He threw up his arms. "If you think it's so easy why not try it yourself? You'll see what I mean."

I smiled.

As soon as I got home, I chucked my work clothes into the laundry room and hit the floor.

I wasn't motivated; I was EXCITED.

Over the next two days, I let excitement over the challenge carry me to the goal.

1,000 pushups. In three days.

I'd tracked my progress in a notebook and texted my cousin the picture.

He texted back immediately:

"Dang. You must be sore…"

That's the thing about doing hard things. Just do it. You see what you want. You make the decision. And you just do it.

I could have wasted so much time getting pumped up listening to music, watching motivational videos on YouTube, or looking at photos of bodybuilders.

Nope. I wanted to spend my time getting what I wanted, not trying to get motivated so I'd follow through.

Competition played a major role of here. Competition made me compare my results with others', then push for better results.

I don't believe motivation is all it's cracked up to be, especially if it takes you in the wrong direction!

Take my decision to drop all that money on real estate education. I got so freaking motivated to do something that, before getting motivated, I wasn't even excited about it. It wasn't a dream I'd carried since childhood, just a fun idea that turned into a season of misery—which I probably should've expected since the guru spent so much effort motivating me to do it.

I wasn't driven then like I was for the pushups. I let the initial emotion of the challenge push me right into the pushups, then kept it going since I'd already started making progress.

Did that feeling subside? You bet it did, and I knew it would. That's why I invested my time in reaching the goal ASAP.

The risk of giving up pushed me once it "got old." *That* is the power of excitement. I didn't need to feel motivated by some external force or person for each and every push-up.

Excitement is what will drive you over the

long-haul.

While beating my cousin was an exciting goal, doing a seven-day challenge in just three was brutal.

The competition is what got me excited.

Maybe we get hung up on the way the gurus, experts, and motivational speakers of the world talk about motivation, as if it's the holy grail of high performance. It's such a forceful word, too—GET motivated.

Contrast that with being excited. Again, one is a state of being, the other is a situational emotion.

You're excited to marry your sweetheart. If you have to "get motivated" to marry your sweetheart, you may need to rethink it.

You're excited for your first day at your dream job. If you have to "get motivated" for your dream job, then perhaps you're in for trouble.

In situations where you feel like you just need to get motivated, your gut instinct is saying, "Hey, I don't really want to do what it is you want to get motivated to do!" It's possible that the task doesn't line up with the vision you have for yourself.

So, what should you be devoting yourself to instead?

Answer to yourself, *what makes me excited?*

Excitement about seeing your dreams, goals, and ambitions become reality will carry you above and through the tough parts of life.

Excitement comes from purpose. In the example, one life purpose I have is to be fit. So that challenge brought excitement because it lead in the direction of my purpose. If you're finding it tough to get excited about anything, check for a purpose. Or, create one.

Whatever the next big thing is in your life, a relationship, a career, a new city, a business venture…focus on the end result you want from it. And whatever excitement you feel, grow it by taking the right action. Right now.

WRITE YOUR OWN CHAPTER

The "next big thing" in your life that excites you:

_____

_____

_____

The vision or purpose this task relates to in your life:

_____

_____

_____

_____

_____

How you will build and sustain the excitement you need to follow through:

_____

_____

_____

_____

_____

ACT WITH TACT

> It's not my place to tell you how to raise your kid, and I'm not telling you that you're wrong. The phrase "Shut Up" is not what you should be telling that girl, she is just a curious angel, how are you going to down a kid like that? Let her have an Imagination, and treat her with the respect that she and every child deserves. It hurts to much to not say something. I hope you understand this is entirely out of love for the girl she could become. Please love her more. Just be patient.
>
> "Thank You, Someone Who Cares.
>
> Have A Nice Day!
>
> PS I know you have that kindness in your heart, after telling me a complete stranger that my braidy was done, these random acts of kindness go farther than you'll ever know, its much appreciated. Thanks.

"Shut up and sit the f*** down! Sit your a** down right now!" This deranged mother screamed at her probably no older than 6-year-old daughter. This went on for more than twenty minutes—twenty minutes that I saw. Who knows what happens at home with no audience.

All that little girl wanted to do was play,

but that interrupted mom's cigarette break.

I listened from a short distance. This woman, who was parked beside me, was belittling and verbally abusing this little girl. And there I sat in my car with a blown mind, wondering why you would treat a small child that way.

On the screaming and cussing went. I glanced around at the other laundromat-goers. Their lack of surprise wasn't surprising. Other than a few awkward glances in the mother's direction, most of the people were "distracted" by newspapers, magazines, or a muted television.

"Distracted" is in quotes, of course, because nobody was really distracted. They just pretended they didn't hear—because they didn't care.

Or maybe they did care about the verbal abuse they could easily have done something about. But they cared more about their own little world and their own little routine.

Let's bring back social responsibility, kids. Too many of us think this kind of behavior is normal because we see it all the time in movies and on TV. On those mediums, such bad behavior doesn't concern us because it isn't real. But the apathy carries over into real life, as we can all see when the mom's kid in aisle three at the grocery throws a tantrum, and the mom retaliates by beating the kid—yet we the shoppers stare on, blinded by our lack of empathy, which by the way…that kid's behavior is a reflection of your parenting skills or lack thereof, but that's another topic.

Those vile words screamed day in and day out at the laundromat kid could cause her to grow up, become a heroin addict, rob someone of their wallet for just another hit, then things go wrong and she guns down her victim—which could be you or someone you love. Who knows!? But why take the chance.

That's what happens when we don't offset the a**holes of this world.

Actually, "being the change you wish to see in the world" comes into play here. This is action, not just reading the quote, mentally agreeing, and continuing life without change.

DO IT!!!!!

A couple of months ago, I was cruising

around the mall in town. There at the main entrance stop sign sat a broken-down car holding up traffic. Angry glares, more than a couple of honks, and a middle finger or two. The man and woman sitting inside the car with their heads down looked pretty rugged, matching the car's state.

As I passed by, I asked if they were okay, and the man spoke right up in a chipper but nervous voice, "Oh yeah, it's fine. Just needs to cool down. Does this all the time!"

I waved and drove around. About fifty feet down the road, I pulled into the adjacent parking lot and put the car in park.

If I have a hundred dollar bill in my wallet, I'm giving it to that couple. I thought. I whipped out my wallet. A one hundred dollar bill.

I doubled back to the couple, pulled over in the lot beside them, ran across traffic, and approached the man.

"Hey, could you use this?" I said.

"Are you seriously giving me money?" Blood rushed from his face.

"Yeah. Could you use this? Use it to fix

the car, get a tow, whatever you want."

His voice lowered. "I can tow it home with this, yeah. You're seriously going to help me because you're that nice of a person." Not a question, more a statement of a fact he wished were true.

"Yeah, we exist." I handed him the cash and shook his hand. "Just pay it forward when you can."

When I walked away from that car, I felt like a million bucks. And that's probably miniscule compared to how they felt. I just wanted to sit in their car with them for the next hour and hear what they had to say. That would be much creepier than walking up to a total stranger and giving them money, so I opted out of implementing that idea.

See, I believe most people are basically good. We just hear about all the a**holes because the s*** they pull gets them on the news. So we have to make it a point to offset their ways, like I said earlier.

Which is why I could not let that mom at the laundromat get off easy.

I ripped out a blank sheet of scratch paper

from my bag and jotted down my thoughts. Once I'd written what she needed—not wanted—to hear, I marched inside and handed it to her.

"This is about your daughter," I said with a stern smile.

"Oh, I know, I'm so sorry. She's a terror. Just a terror. Should've kept her bratty a** at home, let me tell you."

Um. What? Ignorance is not always bliss.

Some folks just don't get it. I hope she did though…'cause here is what I said to her:

It's not my place to tell you how to raise your kid, and I'm not telling you that you're wrong. The phrase "shut up" is not what you should be telling that girl. She is just a curious angel. How are you going to down a kid like that? Let her have an imagination, and treat her with the respect that she and every child deserves. It hurts too much to not say something. I hope you understand this is entirely out of love for the girl she could become. Please love her more. Just be patient.

~ Thank you, Someone Who Cares

Have a nice day!

P.S. I know you have that kindness in your heart, after telling me, a complete stranger, that my laundry was done, these random acts of kindness go farther than you'll ever know. It's much appreciated. Thanks.

If you can do something that is morally right without obviously hurting anyone or anything—don't be an idiot or pretend you're John Wayne headed back to Dodge City. If you could do something or say something—remember, assess the situation first—speak up for what's right.

Speak up for humanity, whether you write a letter or make a phone call or talk to someone directly. And always, do so with tact—don't go and tell them they're wrong, point out what they're doing. See, don't ever fight fire with fire. So the chapter you are writing for your own life here is basically this—when you see someone being an a**hole, put them in check. Help them see what they're doing, help them think about what they're saying or doing.

Just as importantly, point them towards the right behavior, and the right mindset that will help facilitate such behavior—say *what* to do, and *why*. Guide them in a way that will better humanity. Tactful is always more effective than forceful.

WRITE YOUR OWN CHAPTER

How you offset a**holes and restored faith in humanity today:

_____

_____

_____

_____

_____

_____

_____

_____

_____

_____

_____

_____

_____

_____

INVESTING IN DREAMS

Around the time I was finishing up the last round of edits for this book, TIME Magazine featured an article that blasted our generation—the Millennials—calling us "lazy, entitled narcissists."

Maybe that's true about a lot of Millennials.

But I doubt it's true about you.

Now that you've committed to the path of offsetting a**holes, pair it up with offsetting these lazy, entitled narcissists that TIME Magazine has us so worried about.

Stop enabling entitlement.

A great way you can do this is by investing in others' dreams.

Ever since I was a kid, my dad talked over and over about getting a trailer for his truck.

"It'll be my own business on wheels," he'd say.

Maybe it was just fate, but this dream of my dad's never came to pass.

Until I saw his dream as an opportunity. Once little Nathan grew up and landed a big kid job, he began to see his father's dream as a chance to invest in him.

When I was a full year into my first job, I pooled my savings to buy my dad a trailer—his business on wheels. Not only that, but my brother Barry helped me stencil the trailer. Thus, the outside of the trailer was now a moving billboard for his business.

Because I believed in my dad, I invested in his dream.

And because I invested in his dream, my dad gets to enjoy a new element in his life's work he thought was long-forgotten.

When my brother was ready to start his

first big kid job, he needed some serious transportation. There were a couple of small stores within walking distance of home, but that wasn't going to move the needle for him. Because I wanted to see my brother really make something of himself at a young age, I saw another opportunity for investment.

Just days after I helped him with the down payment on his first car, he landed a job well above minimum wage.

All because he now had a way to get there.

A few months later, my brother found an even better position, one that paid even more. 60-minute commute total? No big deal, thanks to the vehicle.

You can bet my brother's total earnings from both of those jobs ridiculously dwarves what I pitched in to acquire the car to make those jobs a possibility for him.

So, what do both of my stories have in common?

I gave them money.

But even though I gave them money, what my father and brother actually got from me was hope.

Belief. Confidence. Opportunity.

I took the chance to jump into investments of the human sort, and it payed off precisely as my father and brother needed them to.

While my examples portray money as the hero, it was merely the beginning of a new opportunity provided.

Paving the way for family and friends to pursue their dreams doesn't always require cash.

What matters most is that whatever you are investing in them be an opportunity, not just a handout that doesn't do anything for them.

I could have paid a few months of my dad's mortgage, but what would that have gotten him? But because his goal was to succeed as his own businessman, I invested in his dream.

For both my dad and brother, the financial resources I committed allowed them to also receive the gift of a work ethic, as in: "Dad, what are you now going to do with your trailer? Brother, what are you now going to go because of that car?"

The goal of all this isn't to show off. Rather, as you look for "human investing" opportunities, you'll find that the ones with the best return aren't advertised.

My dad didn't ask me to buy him a trailer. My brother didn't ask me to pay his first car's down payment.

Because I believed in their dreams and ambitions, my offerings created opportunities for them. If non-monetary resources would have worked as well as cold, hard cash, that's what I would have brought them.

In fact, "sweat equity" can be the most selfless resource you offer to people you believe in.

Know a poor family in the neighborhood who has trouble paying the bills and feeding their kids anything more than fast food?

Get them a fully illustrated, step by step gardening book. Pull some friends together, and go help till a nice square in their backyard to get them started. Help them decide what fruits and vegetables to plant, and let them get to work.

Know a single mom still living at home—and not by her own choosing? Then offer to watch her kid a couple nights a week so she can take evening classes to put her in a position to land a better job and raise her young family independently.

Met a homeless man on the street in the summer heat? Give him a $5 bill to get himself a cold drink—a bill that's stapled to the front of a McDonald's job application.

Okay, maybe that last one didn't quite meet the politically correct standard. My point is, opportunities to invest in our fellow human beings are all around us, if only we had eyes to see and ears to hear about dreams unrealized.

The old cliché cautions, "You can't take it with you."

What does that phrase also imply?

You can leave it behind—with people who will pass it on to even more.

WRITE YOUR OWN CHAPTER

Someone in your life whose dream, ambition, or goal is worth investing in (money or sweat equity):

_____

_____

What one resource, if offered to them, would turn things around:

_____

_____

_____

_____

_____

How you will help them acquire this resource and utilize it to its potential:

_____

_____

_____

_____

_____

MAKE THE MOST

The blazing Guatemalan sun beat down on my pale Ohioan skin, now drenched in sweat from the humidity. I propped my bag of clothes higher up on my shoulder as we neared the remote village. This was my first mission trip, so I had only a little idea of what to expect.

An alleyway behind rundown business and homes led us to a dirt trail down to the river. We were met by pit bulls chained together. Our body guards, hands on pistols, escorted us to our destination.

I couldn't believe it.

Torn trash bags. Rusty sheet metal. A half-dozen different colors of mud.

These were houses. No plumbing, no electricity, no air conditioning.

Men, women, and children of all ages and sizes, most with clothing that looked handmade or hand-me-down.

All of these families exposed to the elements, with no technology in sight.

But they had one thing I rarely see back home—smiles. Bright, genuine, unending smiles. On every child's face.

As we started passing out the clothes to these poverty-stricken people, a small boy, four or five years old, ran up to me and waved at me. I did a double-take. Something on his arm.

You've got to be kidding me...

Tape.

A cassette tape.

This little guy had scavenged for something to play with, and the tape of an unwound cassette was the best toy he could find. No Xbox, Playstation, Wii, or even a ball.

He took off running barefoot in the dirt, scampering around as the other kids chased what remained of the plastic cassette as it dragged behind him. The purest laughter I've ever heard, bar none.

What I witnessed was the furthest thing from materialism. I loved it, every second of it. Not to mention, they were all fit, active kids…

Later, when I jotted down this sight in my journal, I was in total awe. I had a clean sheet of paper. A whole notebook of them. And a pen in my hand that worked so well. I felt gratitude overtake me, gratitude for everything from the clothes I wore to my car, all the way up to family. When you see a kid discovering a toy in a piece of garbage, you realize you've taken pretty much everything for granted.

Think about how much we complain about the tiniest, most insignificant s*** in our lives. The car in front of you doesn't gun it as soon as the light turns green. You have to put the Hot Pocket back in the microwave to nuke its half-frozen center. You can't skip that fifteen-second commercial at the beginning of the YouTube video.

We let these things piss us off, yet if we were forced to live like those Guatemalan villagers for even half a day, I truly believe most of us would crack from modern lifestyle withdrawal. But for all I know, that kid with the cassette tape lives a happier life than I do.

Making the most is really about enjoying where you're at and simply being present. We're living in the future, whether it's anticipating a new game or movie, prepping junk food for the weekend's big game, or staring at the fit chick across the gym just a liiiittle too long, thinking that someday—maybe—you'll build the confidence to go say hi in a non-creepy way.

When you live in the moment and experience contentment with your current place in life, people start to see you differently. For example, my dream car is a sporty two-door that costs over two million dollars. But now when people ask me what my dream car is, I tell them, "A black 2003 Nissan Xterra with 230,000 miles on it."

Not to say I'm totally content with the car

I currently have. I'm happy with it—for now. Don't get me wrong, dreaming, planning, and preparing for the future are awesome. As you know, I'm all for having goals. But I am happy with what I have now as I pursue bigger and better things. The keyword here is "as." This is totally different from being comfortable and complacent, which kills your goals and keeps you stagnant.

It took me that trip to Guatemala to realize that what frustrates some people could make others mind-numbingly happy. It's all about how you perceive the world. Read that golden line again—IT'S ALL ABOUT HOW YOU PERCEIVE THE WORLD.

Speaking of you, it's time to write your own chapter and hit the refresh button on your own perceptions. Here's what you'll do. Put this book down. Right now. Seriously. Right. Now. As soon as you read the next few sentences, that is.

Look around you. Let's face it, probably a lot of boring stuff you see all the time. Focus on ten things right around you that you are thankful for, and write down one reason for each of them why you are thankful.

There's a beautiful world out there, but you'll never be able to see it if you're always wishing for things you don't have. Now open your eyes, and see that you already have everything you could ever need. We all have an unwound cassette tape we've taken for granted far too long. What's yours?

Now.

WRITE YOUR OWN CHAPTER

Ten things you see around you right now that you're thankful for—and why:

_____
_____
_____
_____
_____
_____
_____
_____
_____
_____

Bonus: Go buy a notebook right now and make it your "gratitude journal." These ten are items are just the scratching of the surface.

IF YOU TRUST

I'm suspended fifty-two feet in a shaky man-lift. The rocky ground waaay below. Stomach-turning for those scared of heights.

I look straight out, and there is God himself.

Well, sort of. It's actually Jesus. A fifty-two foot statue, that is.

Back when I worked in exhibit construction, a massive project we had on the table was for a megachurch in the area. They wanted a statue of Jesus overlooking the pond in front of the sanctuary. No biggie.

Building him piece by piece at a shop on ground-level is one thing, but when you're finishing up the head of God more than fifty feet in the air, that's a new game.

Yet the arms were stretched out, a welcoming gesture of comfort.

And for some reason, that's how I felt. High in the air, I was safe because of…God.

The construction lift I was in had a rotating feature, so it could rotate 360 degrees. In the middle of working on the top of the statue, from time to time we'd have to rotate the lift's basket away from the statue and over the dried-up pond. This meant that when I looked down, there was nothing there to catch me. Scary. But when the lift would rotate back into position close to the statue, I felt safe.

Literally.

I was in God's arms.

If the lift toppled over, the Jesus statue would break my fall just a few feet into it.

I saw this as a metaphor for real life. You're out in the world, struggling, maybe feeling like you're about to fall. But God (or the Universe or whatever/whoever you believe in) is there to catch you, or guide you. I know it was a Jesus statue, but I saw it as a symbol of God. As long as you're connected and you have faith and are asking for guidance, you'll understand this almost unexplainable lesson I'm trying to share here.

A few months after the statue experience, when I quit my job, I felt so insecure, so "up in the air." Then I felt God catch me—the new job I easily got earned me in just the first six months what it took me a whole year to make at my previous job. God is good—if you trust.

Back in the days I tried to make the whole college thing work for me, I struggled with an algebra class. Didn't make sense to me and felt like a total waste of time. I hated it.

Then one morning when I merged on to the interstate to head to class, my car skid across the next lane…and the next…and the next. Slammed the wall, totaled the car.

But I was happy. It was like the river of life took me over a waterfall I didn't see coming—and it was exactly the jolt I needed.

"I don't have to go to school!"

I never went back, and life has been great since.

Was the car crash good? Was it bad? Or was it simply…was?

It doesn't matter how I felt about it, because, even in a moment of physical trauma, I knew I was safe in God. Faith that everything would work out guided me to the reality where everything did work out.

So what is it you want? Whatever it is, simply trust that you're headed in the right direction, which will allow you to release worry and stress. Don't judge situations as good or bad because you don't know the ultimate outcome.

In the chapter "Make the Most," you witnessed the simple beauty of gratitude for material possessions. This chapter is similar—as in, making the most of "bad" situations.

Just realize that life is good—because it is. Simply affirm to yourself what you want—and *feel* that you already have it. You become what you think about. So wouldn't you rather think about what you want more than what you don't want?

I affirm myself by saying to myself under my own breath several times a day, "I am energetic, excited, and enthusiastic. I am happy." I want to feel these emotions on a regular basis, so I tell myself that I already feel them—even if I'm having a perfectly s****y day.

So, what do you want to feel? This week? Today? Right now? What emotion do you wish you were feeling? Calm? Joyful? Smart? Confident?

Tell yourself—out loud if possible—that *that* is who you are. Right now. Do it. Use your imagination.

How different would your life be today, tomorrow, the next day, the day after that if you were happy? Confident? Joyful? What would your mornings look like if that is how you felt when you woke up each day? What would your day at work look like? How would you be different around your friends and in your love life? Now go tell yourself who you want to be—and then realize that is who you already are.

WRITE YOUR OWN CHAPTER

3 character / personality traits you want to work towards:

_____

_____

_____

_____

_____

3 affirmations to tell yourself on a consistent basis about the traits you want to embody:

_____

_____

_____

_____

_____

Since speaking these affirmations to yourself daily, how you feel like you're making solid, consistent progress:

_____

_____

_____

_____

_____

_____

_____

_____

_____

UNPLUGGED YET CONNECTED

"Look at that sunrise, man. Just look at it." I looked out at the rising sun one morning, surrounded by co-workers grumbling over coffee. "Beautiful."

"So what?" A grumpier guy said. "Same thing happens every f***ing morning."

How miserable must a man be to make a statement like that?

Why is it so difficult to take just a moment to enjoy nature? Does a sunrise or a sunset really mean anything? I can't even imagine the number of photos I've taken of sunrises and sunsets over the years. I'll probably never go over all those old photos again. But that's okay.

Each time I take a good ten or fifteen minutes to watch the sun rise or fall, my mind is silent. I feel some sort of interconnectedness within the universe, how big our physical world actually is, how we and everything else that exists is totally interdependent on everyone and everything else.

Being totally present, that's where the magic of life happens. Think of the last time you saw a dog, either yours or a friend's. Dogs are totally present, not worrying about the future or regretting past decisions. They simply are.

When you watch a sunrise or sunset, you're just being present, totally aware only of what's happening right now. You're making the most of the moment. Just watch what goes in on nature. The earth's not freaking out, hoping it makes its way around the sun.

So often we recall past emotions, how we felt about he said, what she said, what you should've said. We stop ourselves short of our potential by fretting over that which we can no longer control. Let denial go. Accept what is, and have the will to grow from it. No good, no bad, only life.

When you watch tonight's sunset or tomorrow's sunrise, recall nature's seasons.

In the summer, everything's great and nature grows up nicely.

In the fall, the cycle of life slows down.

In winter, darkness rules, and there's little green to be found.

But come springtime, life blooms for all to enjoy once again.

That's earth; that's life. It doesn't start, it doesn't stop, it's always present. It just is.

Writing your own chapter starts with getting off the couch and heading out into nature.

Go on a walk for one hour outside. No phone. No electronics. Just you. And nature. And listen. Actually listen.

Some of the younger generation who accept this challenge will be bored in less than fifteen minutes because they have nothing to look down to.

When you unplug from technology and connect to nature—even for just a few moments—you are witnessing an ageless and timeless process of life creation and recreation.

Sunrises, sunsets. Summer, winter, fall, spring. Day, night.

All these have existed long before you and I were around to observe them, and they will be around long after we're gone.

So when we take time to honor earth's life cycles and the part we play in them, something happens inside us—we realize who we are really NOT (technology-driven consumers) and wake up to who we truly ARE (participants in the ancient process called LIFE).

Look, technology is a necessity. I'm not saying we should forsake our electronics and return to pre-electricity life. Yet even as we use technology to maintain connections with the people in our lives, we need to keep those relationships grounded in reality.

So are you using technology for something greater than itself, or is it means to its own end?

Whether you go on your tech-free walk in the morning or at night, remember that no number of "likes" for a nature photo you shared can match the wonder of even ten seconds watching the real thing.

Connect with nature and learn from it.

WRITE YOUR OWN CHAPTER

What sights, sounds, and smells you noticed during your walk that you have taken for granted:

_____

_____

_____

_____

_____

Something you learned from nature that can be utilized in your life or career:

_____

_____

_____

_____

_____

THE GRIND

Dirty hands, muscles pumped, sweat-soaked shirt.

Pushing forward, pressing onward, making s*** happen.

This...is the grind.

The grind is where you work for progress and for people, not for paychecks. The grind is where your work has meaning, no matter what you're doing. The grind is where you give 110%, whether you're wearing a tailored three-piece suit or torn up, muddy jeans.

For most people, "the grind" evokes

images of slamming the Monday morning alarm with disgust and disappearing into a lifeless, soul-sucking existence for the day, selling your best eight hours to "The Man."

The struggle is real. But it doesn't have to be for you.

"Thank God it's Friday? I thank God it's *Monday!*"

When your job is monotonous, tedious, or downright dirty, the grind can seem like a bad thing. But if you ask yourself why you're doing that work at that moment, the grind is worth it.

For example, on a recent home inspection I was performing for a client, I had to crawl through dusty, cramped, and humid attic space. It sucked.

Spiders and itchy fiberglass insulation in a space 3 ½ feet tall.

But when I reached the other side of the attic, I found success—there was a leak in the roof, allowing water to seep into the house. In this case, the grind led to catching a potential disaster, which saved my clients money and the headache of finding it later, after even more damage has been done.

When I started my career in the home inspection industry, I was all in...for the money. But now that I've built up clientele, I regularly have people requesting me personally because of the quality and thoroughness I offer. That's what makes nasty crawl spaces worth it. Yeah, the money is a byproduct, but I love helping people and adding value to their lives.

I don't see anything wrong with being selfish, as long as you are serving others first. First you give, then you take. First you work (add value to your employer, co-workers, and customers), then you get paid.

At this point, I know some people are thinking, "Yeah, but you don't understand. If I just work more and get more done, the boss will expect me to keep performing at that level for the same amount of pay. It's a lose-lose scenario, man!"

Really? Don't create bad habits for yourself. Put in that extra effort not because you're gunning for a raise, but because you see yourself as a person who adds value. Plus, you probably won't be there forever—why not leave with the work habits of a top performer who can command a considerable raise elsewhere?

Even if you're working at a restaurant, take pride in serving people. Are you taking a paycheck, or are you giving your time and energy? Are you just taking orders, or are you giving service?

To paraphrase Napoleon Hill, "Let me show you the color of my service. If you like my service, allow me to look at the color of your money."

I've learned both the hard way and the easy way that a person's true value is determined by how much more value they provide to employers, co-workers, and customers than they take in wages.

So embrace the grind. Trust the struggle. And see green—lots of it. Because you'll be worth it.

Time to write your own chapter. This time, you'll actually be writing. Get a notecard and pen. FYI, you're going to be putting this card in your wallet or purse for quick and easy reference going forward.

Write on that notecard 3 things—the 3 things why you do what you do for a career. I'll give you the first one: "To be a better person." The next two can be about your family or your clients and customers or the community, whatever. One caveat—neither can be about money.

Now, every time you fetch money from your wallet or purse, you will see your 3 real reasons for doing what ultimately gets you that money you're about to spend.

Enjoy the fruits of your labor, because no labor done for the right reasons is done in vain.

Just remember what your reasons are.

WRITE YOUR OWN CHAPTER

The 3 real reasons you take on "the grind":

_____

_____

_____

_____

_____

What makes your 3 reasons worth grinding it out every day:

_____

_____

_____

_____

_____

NATURE > CONSEQUENCES

One of my construction projects early in my career consisted of building a parade float to promote recycling. Naturally, I made it out of only recycled materials.

While indeed it was more bada** than any you'll ever see during a homecoming parade, the finished product made me ponder the whole issue of recycling.

Here was some junk slapped together to make something of value to people. But how much trash never gets to be reborn like this?

Just think about what we throw away. Nothing ever actually gets "thrown away."

The packaging that's ten times the size of the tablet or computer it contains—what happens to all that when you pitch it? It's out of sight, out of mind for you as the consumer, but what's happening in the long run is that we're turning planet earth into one giant waste bin. This is the only place our bodies have to live, yet most people don't have a clue what happens to what they throw away. Get educated and join the movement.

You've probably heard the "go green" movement folks talking about leaving no trace, just your positive impact on earth's living creatures. Easier said than done, right?

Not when you begin writing your chapter. First thing I and the world need you to do is watch and be aware of what you buy. SO much useless, short-term used, then trashed s*** lines the shelves of convenience stores. DON'T BUY IT! And be more packaging-conscious. Support the minimal packaging. You're going to get cut opening the well-packaged stuff anyway. That's actually the number-one reason for emergency room visits on Christmas—people cutting themselves while trying to open the junk they got. Seriously, Google it.

The question for you today is, how useful is all the stuff you're buying? Are your purchasing habits focused on lifetime value, or this-looks-cool-I-might-use-it-someday-but-for-now-it-just-takes-up-space?

Buying a new faux tree every Christmas—seriously? Using plastic cups regularly? Why? You think the cheaply made toys and junk that is conveniently placed in the center of ends of the aisle way have any real value? Stop that.

Let's kill this vicious cycle of consuming meaningless s***.

All we have to do is be aware of our purchases—especially when we feel an impulse buy coming on.

Very few impulse buys have value that lasts beyond the day you buy them.

I hope you'll agree—this book is a valuable purchase.

WRITE YOUR OWN CHAPTER

The next time you stop by a supermarket or department store and feel an impulse purchase coming on, ask yourself, "Do *I* need this? Does *the planet* need this?" The next time you face this decision, return to this chapter and record how difficult (or easy) it was to answer these questions:

_____

_____

_____

_____

_____

_____

_____

_____

_____

How you felt *after* leaving the store without making the impulse purchase:

_____

_____

_____

_____

_____

_____

_____

_____

_____

_____

AM I HEADED IN *MY* DIRECTION?

"You realize something, Nathan?" My best friend's mother wagged a finger at my high school senior self. "My generation was the last one that could get away without having a degree!"

She shot a glare at her son, my buddy. "You're going to a university, son. No two ways about it. You need to start thinking about where you want to go in life."

So, young, direction-less me wanted to do the "right" thing, so I hit up the local community college. A placement test, two orientations, and a couple of suggested majors later, I was ready to sign up.

A few days later, my project manager called me into his office. He was a pretty cool guy, so I had no problem throwing my tools onto the bench and leaving my project in the shop for a talk with him.

"So, you're getting ready for college?" He asked. More of a statement of fact though.

"Yeah, seems like it." I shrugged.

"Going to college fits with your life goals, doesn't it? 'Cause I think it would at least fit with our plans for your advancement here."

To a high school kid lusting after real paychecks, of course I wanted in. "Well yeah, absolutely it does!"

"You know, our draftsman is getting pretty old. 63 next spring, I believe. Anyway, I figure that by the time he retires, you will have gotten your degree in industrial drafting and designing, so you'll be ready to take over for him."

I'd only met the drafter once. A short conversation we had. I dropped by his cubicle once. And seeing him buried in piles of paperwork and glued to three computer monitors, I shrugged and headed back to the shop floor.

I glanced down at the floor, then back up at my project manager. "Okay." I shrugged.

"Fine!" He got up, slapped me on the back, and walked me to the shop while shooting lame, half-baked jokes about getting good grade and college girls.

Easier said than done, boss.

I had no actual interest in the matter, which made the classes boring and miserable.

Because I had outsourced my decision—"College or career?"—to people who I thought knew better, I'd put myself at the mercy of their decision.

First, my math teacher had the thickest Russian accent I'd ever heard. Looking back, maybe she actually was speaking Russian. Either why, it sucked.

Class, failing.

Then, I tried my freshman luck at blueprint design. They must have dragged the poor instructor out of the old folks' home and duct-taped him to a desk, because every few words, he gasped for his breath as if it were about to be his last.

I did good here because I knew the material. But still, I felt miserable.

It wasn't long before I was asking myself the question I bet 99.99% of hopeful freshmen ask:

"Why am I even here?"

Honestly, looking back, I should have known better. I'm not a sit-behind-the-computer type of guy. Just give me a hammer, and let me go.

I realized I was biting the bullet for other people whose opinions I valued more than I should have.

Last generation, my a**.

As you read in several earlier chapters, it took a nasty car wreck for me to wake up and quit school. My hope is that you don't need a car wreck of your own to literally stop you from heading in the wrong direction.

That moment of relief behind the wheel of my totaled car changed my course. I was trying to fit into someone else's vision of my life.

So I shut out all the voices in my head, dropped out of every class, and dove headlong into my career.

I was totally okay with this because I became self-aware; aware of who I wasn't—college material—and aware of who I truly was—a craftsman.

Don't ride someone else's wave. Look at what you're doing with your life, the choices you're making. Why are you doing those things and making those choices? Are they in line with your strengths, or are you pretending that one day you'll conquer your weaknesses and then build off of those? Life is far too precious to waste it not building on your actual strengths.

Hopefully it doesn't take something drastic like a car wreck to help you reach that level of self-awareness.

Be real with yourself. And be blunt. Make choices—big decisions and the little ones—based on who you know you are, versus what others think you should do or what you wish you could do.

Your direction is…?

WRITE YOUR OWN CHAPTER

Who you are as a person and what defines you:

_____

_____

_____

_____

_____

Suggestions from others that can sway you away from who you are:

_____

_____

_____

_____

_____

What you are going to do about it:

_____

_____

_____

OPEN MIND, OPEN WORLD

"Hey, I know her!" I said to myself while scanning a featured blog on rock climbing.

The theme—female rock climbers taking charge in a male-dominated sport. A photo at the top of the article was of a girl who worked at the indoor rock climbing facility in town.

Right about now would be a good time to let you know that I'm not the ladies' man (aka, a "player"). Thus, my interactions with her so far didn't even border on flirty—which made what happened next even stranger.

Whilst mindlessly browsing my Facebook feed I messaged her a congratulations, which started a normal conversation all about climbing. Then, I spotted a status update of hers.

"So my best friend and I were going to go to Colorado for 8 days, but she just got in a car wreck and can't go. It would suck to go by myself, so would any of you friends like to go with me?"

I replied in our thread, "Colorado, huh? That's sweet, sounds like fun."

An immediate reply, "You should go."

Wait—what? Go with her? Somebody I barely knew?

"We don't really know each other that well," I wrote right back.

"It's an eighteen-hour drive. We can bond."

I'd be an idiot to say no at this point.

So, over the next forty-eight hours, I met her up at the park for a hike so we could no longer call each other just acquaintances, and then I stopped by her parents' house to meet her folks. No dad wants their daughter driving halfway across the country with some dude from the rock climbing gym whom he's never met.

Before we left on the trip, we'd hung out for a total of about four hours. So I guess you could say things were getting pretty serious...................................

Over the eight-day trip, we hit up six national parks, drove well over 2,000 miles, and slept in sleeping bags beneath the stairs pretty much every night.

You can probably figure out that she was right—we bonded.

Pretty quickly.

So many memories.

It was epic.

Probably the most memorable part of the trip for me was driving across the US and back. Man, that shows you how tiny our own little worlds are in our hometowns. Made me think on a grand scale, too—our planet is ridiculously small within this vast universe.

Earth's seven billion people, standing shoulder to shoulder, could all fit in the city limits of Los Angeles, California. All seven billion people. That's 7,000,000,000! And then some.

Have you observed the people around

you who feel stuck in meaningless routines? They go to the same place of work, say the same "hey how are you's" to the same co-workers, go to the same restaurants, grab the same beer with the same group of friends stuck in the same grind as you, watch the same TV shows even though they've sucked for the past four seasons, and check in to the same social media sites to share the same memes. Such is a life without spontaneity. Sound familiar?

Our time is just so important! Look how rigid our schedules are. Wake up, breakfast, exercise, shower, commute, meetings, projects, lunch, meetings, projects, commute, dinner, video games, TV, bed. Sound familiar? One thing after the next with little breathing room. What's really happening here is that we're scheduling ourselves into boredom and sterilizing our imaginations!

When we were little kids and had to take a sick day off from school, we played with our favorite toys, read our favorite books, and made our favorite crafts to pass the time. Minus how crappy we felt, it was basically a vacation. Now when we take sick days off from work and have no clue what to do with ourselves except watch *The Price Is Right* accompanied by Life Alert and "diabeetus" commercials.

What the heck are you doing with your life, kids?

Our minds stay so closed when we close ourselves off from the outside world. Rarely do we just up and drive a state or two away to explore a new city and "culturize" ourselves. Yeah, it's fun to do this, but what's the real payoff for doing so? You'll see the world from a fresh perspective, make quality connections, and take away ideas to make your life and community even more enjoyable. Sounds like a win-win-win to me.

That being said, it's time to write your own chapter and unleash that inner spontaneous streak that's been buried by schedules, obligations, and responsibilities.

Here's what you do. Pick a city, a landmark, whatever that's in another state you've never been to. And just go. This weekend (or whenever you get at least two days off from work in a row). Find some locals and talk to them. Get a feel for how these people live. If you don't want to talk, just watch them. People act differently in different places. Observe the actions and habits of other people who don't live quite like you to expand your horizons.

Check out the buildings and businesses. So much is different from the town you know.

For example, when I ventured from Dayton, Ohio to Toronto, Canada, I was met with instant culture shock. The locals were friendly to tourists like me. When I was there, I ran into a Canadian family who took twenty minutes out of their day to share all the joys their city had to share with newcomers.

The prices weren't so friendly though—a crash course in the Canadian economy. The architecture, from downtown offices to the suburban neighborhoods, displayed all different shapes and styles. A huge contrast from my hometown.

Got monotony? Go travel. It's time to find out where your own personal Colorado

is.
Then, just go.
Expand.
Live.

WRITE YOUR OWN CHAPTER

The two-states-away city to visit:

_____

_____

_____

_____

_____

Why you chose that city:

_____

_____

_____

_____

_____

What are 3 ways that city's culture is similar to your hometown's, and 3 ways it's different:

_____

_____

_____

_____

_____

ONLY SO MUCH

"Finders keepers."

It was smack-dab in the middle of nowhere in rural Arkansas that I learned how profitable the old catchphrase could be for me.

Pike County, Arkansas. Crater of Diamonds National Park. A raw diamond mine open to the public. Shovels and buckets provided. Finders keepers.

As soon as my brother Barry and I heard about this gem of a national park (pun intended) on a Sunday, we couldn't get there fast enough. We threw our gear into his car after work the very next day and made the trek there.

This place was basically an open, muddy field without crops. It didn't look at all like a mine.

We dicked around for hours searching for the perfect spot, not sticking around in one place for more than a few minutes before switching to another area.

And still we searched. Maybe that spot over by the woods? Nah, too many trees and bushes to get through. What about digging deeper in existing holes started by other tourists?

We spent as much time "looking" for a so-called perfect spot, we hardly did any actual "digging." I've since realized that you can't find the diamonds of life by "looking."

While we didn't hit the find of the century, we only dug up a few pieces of quartz not worth keeping.

Life is like a diamond mine. This particular diamond mine, at least. See, we spent so much time walking around looking for just the right spot to dig, that I didn't do any digging. I wasted so much time looking for just that right spot.

In life, we spend so much time waiting for the right timing that the moment we wanted so desperately to take full advantage of is long-gone. Maybe you waited a half-hour too long to talk to the hottie winking at you from across the coffee shop. While you were busy coming up with the least lame pickup line, she gathered up her things and just walked out. Perhaps you and your buddy always planned to start a business together. But all you ever did was talk about how great it would be someday.

"But it just wasn't the right time! It wouldn't have worked out!" we tell ourselves to feel better. But let's cut the BS here.

You know what these excuses are?

Distractions.

Get them out of your life, today.

Let's write your life's next chapter and take action to guarantee we won't ever let those opportunities slide on by us. We can start small.

Dial down on your daily routine. Even

what you did today. Examine it closely. How much time did you waste? Maybe you checked Facebook thirteen times, texted your buddies aimlessly about last night's game, or played some useless smartphone games.

Take into account even all the little things.

So here's the challenge. If we do things right on a small scale, those habits transfer to the big tasks in life. On your next set of errands to the store, buy a stopwatch. It'll be no more than two or three bucks. On Sunday (or whatever day you have the least amount of work and family obligations), you're going to time every time-wasting activity you do. I'm talking the non-essential s*** here, like scanning your Twitter feed, binge-watching Netflix, or hitting up the gas station down the street to buy junk food.

Seriously.

Time all of this.

But here's the caveat. Don't keep that timer in your pocket or coat or even somewhere next to you. Put it front and center. Mindlessly perusing your smartphone apps while chilling on the sofa?

Set the timer in your lap while you do so.

Flip through random channels until you find a not-half-bad movie that you won't even finish?

Set the timer next to your TV facing you.

Shuffling off to get junk food from the pantry you've already checked fifteen times today?

Carry the timer in your hand.

While the goal from the start is not for you to adjust your routine—it's to track it—soon you'll realize that you hold your time, no, your very life in your hands. And you're wasting it on purposeless activities that won't matter by tomorrow morning. Knowing this should make you want to adjust your routine.

I'm not saying it's bad to watch TV or just chill out with your buddies, so don't feel like you should go completely cold turkey. Simply realizing that you spend X number of hours and Y number of minutes on non-essential stuff will (or should) motivate you to change what you do and eliminate the "time" excuse.

Instead of watching four or five episodes of that Friends marathon, hold yourself to just one. And remember, keep the timepiece handy.

Once you've accounted for all of these hours you've wasted and have now decided to cut back, choose to spend those hours differently from now on.

Instead of that extra hour of TV that doesn't get you anywhere, go spend an hour socializing with real, live people. Make connections that will make your life better, just something productive.

You only have so much time. Spend it wisely.

WRITE YOUR OWN CHAPTER

Hours you spent wasting your life:

_____

_____

_____

_____

_____

What you're going to do with your time next week:

_____

_____

_____

_____

_____

Come back one year from today. How life has improved since you started using time wisely:

_____

_____

_____

_____

KEEP THE PLANT RUNNING

If you Google the word "focus", you're going to get more results than there are people in the United States.

It's time to experience "the flow state"— an experience of focus where your best work, your best results, and your best "you" exist.

How are we ever going to engage in our life's work if we get caught up in stopping and restarting what we should really be getting done every single day?

When I received full sets of instructions, drawings, or blueprints for what my employer's finished project needed to look like, I went right to work.

Sketching, measuring, cutting, building. No stopping me. Day after day after day, immersed so deeply in my craft. No concept of breaks or quitting time.

I worked each phase until it was completed, keeping my thoughts always on that next step—where am I going with this, why, and what will it look like?

It was because this flow state came easy to me on wire-to-wire projects that my salary was twice what most people my age made.

But on the opposing side, I received direction from my supervisor for other projects that amounted to, "Just go as far as you can on this, and I'll let you know when we get the go-ahead to start planning the next phase of the work. Until then, just go work on other projects around the shop."

Jumping to another project right in the middle of one will cause your "time to work-done" ratio to drop. You may still make forward progress, but it's not ideal and you're not at peak performance.

Since I didn't have an obvious "bullseye"

for the work I was doing, where was I supposed to throw my darts of focus?

If I'm switching from random project to random project, not allowing myself to ever rise into the flow state, am I really making significant progress?

Remember, a state of constant stopping and restarting drains more energy than maintaining productivity does.

The business magazine Fast Company cited a study showing that, every time to get interrupted, it takes just over 23 minutes to refocus on your task.

Here's a real-world example of this phenomenon.

There's a prominent concrete company near my hometown that runs 24/7/365. No holidays off, no closing times, no stopping just to make a repair.

Their reasoning? It takes so much electricity, fuel, and manpower to restart all the equipment once it's stopped, that it's much, much cheaper to never stop in the first place.

In your own "concrete factory"—your

career, your studies, your hobbies, your relationships—what really needs to get going and keep going?

Time for your day's challenge.

Take the side project you're working on. Or the promotion at work you're gunning for. Or the potential lover you're desiring to woo.

Work on it.

Just it.

And only it.

WRITE YOUR OWN CHAPTER

What result you envision getting out of your side project (or relationship, career move, college class, etc.):

_____

_____

_____

_____

_____

Distractions that pop-up when you begin making progress:

_____

_____

_____

_____

_____

"CHECK IN" TO REAL LIFE

On a recent home inspection for my job, I was in a hundred year-old plus house. The home's seller looked to be nearing the same age. At any rate, she was in the process of moving her stuff out when I and the buyer showed up.

I asked her about all her belongings, how she planned to move them, whether she'd secured a mover, etc. She shifted from toe to toe, and quietly let out that she had a friend with a pickup truck—and a bad back.

So, I volunteered to help her move her

stuff. For free. No strings attached. No next-day invoices.

Just be a good neighbor. She seemed scared to ask for help, but I believe people are willing to help. And who knows, maybe the favor will be returned.

You can have fans, followers, and friends on social media, but the community I'm referring to is the real-life connections around you. Building community literally means to build up those around you.

Community service projects can be great, but authentic relationships are built through spontaneous adventures that you're <u>not</u> asked to undertake by an organization.

You help because you want to help.

You meet a need because you see a need.

You build your community because it's *your* community.

This doesn't only mean lending a helping hand. Sometimes, it's doing a favor for the greater society.

A local park I hike and bike at several times a week is home to ancient fossil fields—as well as some rather modern weekend parties.

Young kids party it up after closing time and leave the place a ravage mess, chucking leftover beer cans and trash everywhere.

You meet a need because you see a need.

Now, occasionally when I exercise there, I carry empty garbage bags with me to drag pound after pound of trash back to the parking lot.

Remember, seeing a need and taking care of it benefits everyone. An excuse like, "That's the park rangers' job," wouldn't have been acceptable.

It's not like I did something Nobel Prize-worthy. Sometimes, a helping hand can make all the difference.

Every year, I help a family in my community renovate their house. I don't get paid for it, and the work is the definition of monotonous. But, I enjoy it.

There's no feeling quite like it, pursuing selflessness. It's a bliss you can't get when trading labor for money.

When I helped build greenhouses in Guatemala, my responsibility consisted of toting massive buckets of wet cement to and from the construction site.

In the middle of the day.

In 110 degree heat.

The time of my life—no joke.

Today's challenge won't necessarily require such discomfort, but I can guarantee you will see the people around you in ways you've not seen before—as a community.

A community with needs.

And a community whose needs *you* can help meet.

One moving box, one trash bag, one cement bucket at a time.

WRITE YOUR OWN CHAPTER

If you've already done a selfless service to people in your community, write what you did and how you felt doing it:

_____

_____

_____

_____

_____

If not, come back when you noticed a need and met it. Write down how you felt while doing it:

_____

_____

_____

_____

_____

DON'T BE A STRANGER

When I was on the missions trip to Guatemala, one of our assignments was to pass out used clothes to the villagers stricken with poverty. Once we reached the trail head of this riverside village, a group of skinny, under-developed preteen kids rushed toward our group.

Wow, they must really be excited to try all these on, I thought. But they did something incredible instead.

"Let us carry the clothes for you," the tallest girl said in Spanish.

The size of the bags was larger than the

kids themselves. And here they were, more grateful than I to be able to share with their family and friends the middle class American hand-me-downs or clothes many of us would just pitch.

Kindness for kindness, smiles for smiles, gratitude for gratitude.

Here in everyday life, I think sometimes we take for granted those small steps other people take out of their way simply to be kind. It is vitally important that we recognize these because it makes life fun! It is so worth focusing on the good things in life, no matter how small, especially in a culture that seems to glorify bad things that happen. It used to be a common courtesy to write thank-you notes, for instance. Whether for a party, a small gift, or helping a neighbor out with yard work, letters expressing genuine gratitude once were the norm for random acts of kindness.

Which is why one particular thank-you note I received meant more to me than my high school diploma.

When I visited my friend's high school graduation party, I brought the standard gift—cash, $20 worth. I didn't expect a thank-you note, of course, since I hadn't known this girl that long. Yeah, I gave her a listening ear and advice on life when she was struggling with school and family issues, but isn't that what real friends do?

To her, this was above and beyond. No more than half a week after my friend's graduation party, I received a letter from her in the mail.

A generic thank-you card.

The second I opened it, I smiled.

Top to bottom, both sides of the note—all filled with heartfelt appreciation. I read it multiple times, and still to this day read it every now and then.

Oh Nathan, I could seriously write you a book with how much I have to say to you. #1, thank you for the money, even though you know how I feel about it haha. #2 THANK YOU FOR EVERYTHING. Though we haven't known each other that long, you are one of the most amazing people-person guys I've ever met. You have been there for me more than I could have asked and one of the most incredible friends in the world. I really hope everything goes well with your real-estating and you'll have to keep me updated! Keep up your adventures and I know you're going to do super great with everything. We will have to get Chipotle sometime. DON'T be a stranger!

She was grateful. And I was grateful, even more because knowing I made a positive impact on another's life is worth waaay more than $20.

This is an unending cycle, a snowball effect of kindheartedness.

We hear a lot of people in the media drone on about finding your purpose, following your bliss, pursuing your passions, and so on. When it comes down to it, our purpose is simple—to help others in the unique way each of us are able. The sooner you get on the cycle of gratitude, thoughtfulness, and authenticity, the sooner you'll realize you don't have to discover you're purpose—because you're already living it.

That's what the good life is all about—making a positive impact on other people.

Just like my friend did (and made my day),

write your own chapter by writing a thank-you card. A real, hand-written thank-you card. Go make somebody else's day by filling that card up. Target someone who has had a lasting impact on your life, like a friend, mentor, professor, whatever. Maybe that person didn't even do something they considered all that grand, but it meant the world to you, as was the case with my friend.

So what are you waiting for? Your purpose is waiting for you—and it's a $0.49 stamp away.

WRITE YOUR OWN CHAPTER

Transcribe the note here OR fold up a copy of the note you sent and slip it into the book:

_____

_____

_____

_____

_____

_____

_____

_____

_____

_____

_____

_____

_____

_____

ENDLESS LEARNING

A book? Or a toy?

A book? Or a toy?

For your average middle class American kid, when facing the decision of reading a book or playing with a toy, the preferred choice is blindingly obvious.

But to a youngster who sleeps every night on a dingy rag in a clay hut, to a boy who has to walk five miles twice daily to fetch a small bucket of fresh water for his younger siblings, to a child who doesn't even know how old he is because both parents died of an easily treatable bacterial infection, the choice is obvious.

Even if he can't read.

Because knowledge is more than power. Knowledge is a poverty-breaker.

When I travelled to Guatemala several years ago, my mission was to help a local faith-based team build a school for the children of a remote rainforest village. Little did I know that I would be the one to learn a lesson.

When the team I worked with handed out a bunch of toys and books, nearly every single kid reached for a book first.

Anyway, those kids in Guatemala valued not simply the books, but what the books represented—the spirit of lifelong learning. Like those kids in the village, we should always be willing to learn more, to be teachable at all times. When I was a kid, I guarantee I'd always choose the toy—any toy—over a book. But why? Being raised in an age of prevalent materialism, why not? Stuff brings happiness, right? Nope. Stuff amuses us as a distraction from our journey to discover what truly brings us happiness.

There is more to life than toys (video games, another round of drinks at the bar, a new sports car, in-ground swimming pool, etc.). Knowing, growing, and learning are—and always should be—more important.

Don't get me wrong, I'm all for nice, useful things when you can afford them. Don't stretch yourself or sugarcoat your financial situation. Be smart about it.

With knowledge, you can acquire skill. With skill, you can create. And when you create, you give life to your dreams.

When I say growing, I mean growing of the mind. Stretch it with the imagination that comes with learning new things. It's a simple process as well as enjoyable. Ever see something being made that fascinated you? You couldn't remove your gaze you were so mesmerized. Take note of those moments and dig deeper to explore that feeling. Think in terms of how you can better yourself and society with the activity that deeply interests you.

When it comes to learning, tackle subjects that interest you. Traditional school subjects bored me to no end, so that's not the type of learning I mean. I was a C-student at best until my junior and senior years of high school when I attended a tech school to study carpentry, which was something I actually enjoyed.

Since you're reading this, you don't have a problem with learning. In fact, you probably enjoy picking up new strategies, learning fresh info, and trying new things.

But sometimes we feel like we don't know enough. Just have to figure this thing out first before jumping. Only one more piece of information to get, then I'll be ready to take the leap! I just don't feel ready yet. It doesn't seem like it's good timing for that right now, you know?

These are the sorts of things we think and say when we're caught on the hamster wheel of endless learning.

We can never know it "all." >>> That's right, so why waste time waiting and not taking action with what you already know?

Just have to learn one more thing first before jumping.

Only one more piece of information to get, then I'll be ready to take the leap. >>> Take action right here, right now with what you have right in front of you.

I just don't feel ready yet. >>> Richard Branson says that what sets billionaires apart from everyone else is that they leap into pursuing their big ideas long before they ever feel prepared.

It doesn't seem like it's good timing for that right now, you know? >>> So sometime in the future will/might be a better time? How do you know you're going to have a tomorrow? I guarantee that if you tell yourself (and other people) this excuse, progress in life will be slow.

In the chapter on pursuing our big ideas, we talked about putting some skin in the game. For me, that came when I realized, "Oh s***, I just bought this house! Guess that means I have to fix it up and sell it."

Now, I'm not going to insult you for struggling with endless learning or make fun of you for your notebook filled with business ideas you never acted on. But I am going to throw down a challenge.

Time to write your own chapter. Today, let's have some fun with the transition from "student mode" where we feel we just have to learn one more thing, to "apprentice mode," where we learn by doing.

After completing this challenge, you will be able to show off that skill, talent, or whatever you've always wanted to brag about.

Whatever the thing is that you just never quite got around to doing, but have spent hours and hours learning, today is the day it changes.

So is tomorrow.

And the day after.

And so on.

What is it you've been studying or trying to learn? Maybe it's ballroom dancing or woodworking.

You've nurtured a genuine interest, and you know enough to get started—but you haven't yet.

Those dance shoes are neatly in the package; the hammer shows no signs of wear.

Why?

The point of learning is not to learn, the point of learning is to do, then keep learning more as you *do* more.

That is the sweet spot of lifelong learning, as opposed to the trap of endless learning.

Learning for learning's sake is to be stuck in a vicious cycle that looks and feels productive but produces nothing.

For example, I got stuck in a state of, "But I don't know enough yet," when I invested and reinvested in the real estate training. I knew enough to buy, fix, and sell my first property before I even attended the training.

If you keep saying, "I just have to know this one thing first," you may very well find yourself in the hole $40k without anything to show for it.

If you're an aspiring woodworker, build your first shelf. Or stool. Or shadowbox. Whatever.

Just start. Once you've started, keep going. If you run into something that you don't know how to do, find one tutorial to solve that one problem, then move on.

You may get the feeling that you need to stop and learn more first.

Don't.

Keep going.

Just keep going.

You'll learn more through action than through reading.

WRITE YOUR OWN CHAPTER

What you have watched, studied, or learned about but never started:

_____

_____

_____

_____

_____

Begin lifelong learning by starting to do. Where you will start:

_____

_____

_____

_____

_____

STORIES WORTH WRITING, STORIES WORTH READING

"See, you put all the mixed fruit in the blender," my co-worker Zach said. "Oh, make sure it's tropical. Pineapples and mangoes and stuff. Then you dump in all the vodka. And, *boom*, you've got yourself some jungle juice. The ladies love it!"

"Cool." I nodded, forgetting most of what he said seconds after he finished.

That was the thing about this guy. You'd figure "part-time employee" meant he worked only part of the time he was there. Story after story of the glory days of his youth—acid trips, midnight clubbing, drinking games—filled up his schedule.

"Hey Nate!" Zach yelled at me as he walked towards the workshop exit for another smoke. "Write that s*** down!"

*Write that s*** down…*

From that moment onward, every time one of my co-workers told a funny story, shared a wild experience, reminisced about the good ole days, or gave me half-baked advice for a "successful" life, some joker yelled out from the shop floor, "Hey Nate! Write that s*** down!"

Their good ole days didn't continue like they planned, and the tips for a happy life, well…consider the source.

I wasn't about to write any of THAT s*** down.

But for whatever reason, I started writing s*** down anyway.

And when I started sharing my stories, musings, philosophies, and general life observations, I started sharing them with people—and they got inspired.

Look, just because someone—even me—

writes something, doesn't mean it's worth reading, or that it even merits writing in the first place. Most books published these days sell fewer than 100 copies.

But books that inspire…books that challenge…books that influence…

Those are books I want to read (and should be shared).

And that's the kind of book I wanted to write.

I'm nobody special or privileged. I just want to nudge you in a better direction, one where you are in control.

The idea that keeps crossing your mind.

The opportunity that comes around and around again.

The feeling that creeps deeper into your mood daily.

Stories of inspiration nudged me down the path of authorhood, not just because my stories were worth sharing, but because I believe *yours* are worth sharing, too

Look, the people I want reading this book are those who want more for their lives, who want to make a difference, who want to leave humanity—this planet even—a better place than how they found it.

The stories of future world-changers like you are worth sharing—every step of the way. The epic life is worth writing about, and it's worth living.

The act of telling just one story can be the nudge that causes the dominoes of inspiration and action to fall in another's life.

Several folks I've met over the years who became authors told me that, when they announced to the world they were writing a book, got the universal response, "Oh, cool. I want to read it. When's it coming out?"

That's not why I wrote this book—to get people to buy it.

When I told friends of mine about my book-writing journey, I got <u>exactly</u> the response I wanted.

"So…what do you think?" I closed my 3-hole punch notebook after reading a chapter of my then-work in progress. "Did you like it?"

"Dude!" Chad shook his head. "That's amazing! People need to hear this."

The next morning, Chad texted me:

"Dude, you really inspired me to start my own book. I've been wanting to do this for a long, long time. I'm on a roll!"

When I told my buddy Brent I was working on my first book, he cut me off mid-sentence, "Hey, that's crazy…I've been writing a book for awhile now, too."

2 days later, Brent called me with the news, "You've inspired me, man. I'm writing 2,000 words a day, and there's no stopping me. No looking back. I'm busting this book out!"

A few weeks later, I hit up the local dojo to see my friend Scott. When I shared one of this book's stories with him from memory, his eyes widened, "Are you kidding me!? I've always wanted to write a book, too!" He smiled. "Now I have an excuse to finally get started."

All 3 people had the same response. It wasn't, "Oh, cool. I want to read your book." It was, "Oh, cool. I want to write my own."

I realized that life should be worth writing—and therefore reading—about.

We should leave the next generation with better stories. Share your dreams and goals with others to set them free to pursue theirs.

That is why I write.

My goal is to help you achieve yours.

My dream is to help you believe in yours.

My story is to help you write and share yours.

That's why you've gone through the Write Your Own Chapter sections in this book—to effectively write your own stories-worth-remembering as you've living them, day by day.

If you—yes, YOU—are the only person inspired by this book to dream greater dreams and set bigger goals, then the book is a success. So the fact that 3 different people made a decision to take on their own dreams and goals before I even finished, published, and printed this book…well, that's a humble brag on my part.

Because we're wrapping things up—and you have the paradox of a Conclusion waiting for you next—there's nothing to write down in this chapter.

But there is something I want you to write down.

In your heart.

In your spirit.

In your consciousness.

What can *your* stories do for people? Who out there is waiting to be inspired by you? How can you make our world a happier, healthier, more fulfilled, and more peaceful world by sharing your stories with the people who need the "nudge" they provide?

Now, go.

Write that s*** down.

CONCLUSION: YOUR INTRODUCTION

Over the past month or so, you've acted on your ideas, undertaken the journey of endless learning, kicked fear out, and improvised like crazy.

But everything you've done—from "writing your own chapters" to tackling the exercises—has been merely the training wheels.

Consider this book your orientation for the real deal. Learning lessons is a lifelong process.

That's why this is the last book you'll ever write.

A life that isn't worth writing about is hardly worth living. Pretty harsh, but true. But with this book, you've chosen a different path. You've read the sample stories (mine) and, through each chapter you've "written" one of your own.

Now you're done with this book and the action steps.

You've spent weeks now on a journey toward greatness. Just as I learned through the lessons in my own stories, you have likewise learned how to take on the next task, but smarter.

As with any crowd, there will be people who read this book and get fired up…only to forget everything a week later.

Look, I couldn't care less about whether anybody remembers my stories. Here's why.

When you were a kid figuring out a new, really hard math problem, what did you do first? You read over a couple of examples to get the hang of it, master the new concept, and—voila—you were able to tackle your own math problems and get to the right answer.

How much credit did you ever give to the sample problems? Probably not a whole lot. And that's the point. They served their purpose—show you how to find your right answer. The principles are the point.

That's why this book includes my stories—they're merely samples for you to discover ways to achieve mastery in different areas of your own life. If I can be a conduit to helping people become who they were always meant to be—fired up, awakened to their purpose, getting s*** done, standing for a cause, solving real problems—I did my job.

My hope is that, through "writing your own chapter" at the close of each of my stories, you have begun finding answers to the question, what makes you come alive?

And remember, you don't have to go out and save the entire planet. All you have to do is better one tiny little part of it, one day at a time, using the skills, interests, and abilities you already have. Chances are, you uncovered and began to hone some new ones through writing your own chapters with the pen of life experiences.

Whether you're meeting people, traveling abroad, excelling in your career, starting a small enterprise in your garage, or making our planet a more fertile place, your life is one worth living.

Because you're alive.

You have the confidence to think for yourself because you realize what you're capable of.

You can be the one who takes whatever abilities you have and get done what needs to get done.

You can be the one who acts on your idea, however big or small, to move one step at a time closer to your grand vision.

You can be the one who acts with tact to bring justice to those with no voice.

You can be the one who greets the stranger and makes them feel welcome in your community.

You can be the one who lets a creative spark ignite your imagination and unleash your ability to build whatever you can dream of.

You can be the one who separates

distractions from the diamonds of life, moments where you realize how precious your time is.

You can be the one who sees the wisdom of collecting knowledge and chooses the path of endless learning over fleeting entertainment.

You can be the one who is ever so grateful for the underappreciated people all around you—and shows it.

You can be the one who finds yourself in the darkest, scariest depths of life where others give up.

You can be the one who gets off the sidelines and show your friends how happy a person can be when they dance like no one's watching.

You can be the one who treasures the relief of honesty and the power of karma as you walk a path of integrity.

You can be the one who kicks fear by standing face-to-face with terror, never flinching until your opponent steps down.

You can be the one who improvises a plan in the moment to save the project when the original plan didn't work.

You can be the one who makes a decision to take the lead when so-called authorities abdicate their responsibilities.

You can be the one who makes the most of whatever you've been given, no matter how tiny or seemingly insignificant it is.

You can be the one who does your part to protect our one planet and its ability to sustain life.

You can be the one who finds safety in God by affirming who you are—the real you who has no fear, feels no hesitation, and bows to no one.

You can be the one to jump on the joy of spontaneity, where your imagination is your destination and you discover yourself through the unfamiliar.

You can be the one who is present for the sunrise and sunset, who savors an awareness of your place in an eternal universe.

You can be the one who works the grind hard—and makes the grind work even harder for you.

You can be the one with a work ethic that

gets you promoted to levels far beyond yours peers.

Yes, you can be the one—the one you were always meant to be. Whether you believe in that sort of thing or not.

And along the way, write everything down. Record your stories and life experiences.

That way, when tough times hit—and if you live on planet earth, it will—you will be able to immediately refer back to what you've written in the pages to come and remind yourself who you are.

Write down your victories, the painful lessons you've learned, and even just plain funny stories of times you learned something new about yourself.

Our generation has to pass on better stories.

But first, we have to create them.

We have to live them.

Our culture is saturated with tales of bad news, disasters, dysfunction, crime, destruction, and war.

What would it mean to your kids, your

grandkids, your great-grandkids even, to have a masterpiece journal filled with stories of their ancestor—who they were, what epic lives they lived, which lessons they learned along life's path, and how they made this world a more fulfilling place?

Why not find out by turning the blank pages that follow into a volume of epic stories of your own, day by day?

You've come this far. The training wheels are off. My examples are out of the way.

So start living.

Start writing.

Never stop.

ABOUT NATHAN KESSLER

A carpenter from the two-stoplight farm town of Arcanum, Ohio. Projects have included a life-size model space shuttle and a 52-foot tall statue of Jesus Christ.

A dreamer with the vision of making the world a better place by sharing stories worth hearing and reading.

Stories that inspire. Stories that awaken. Stories that challenge us to think deeper, laugh longer, and live larger.

These stories are worth writing, and stories worth *living*.

What are your stories? You're already living them <u>now</u>. Are they worth reading?

Share yours at
www.TheLastBookYoullEverWrite.com

NATHAN KESSLER